The Bread Machine
Cookbook

Donna Rathmell German

Bristol Publishing Enterprises, Inc.
San Leandro, California

A Nitty Gritty® Cookbook

Printed in the United States of America.

ISBN 1-55867-025-4

Cover design: Frank Paredes
Cover photography: John Benson

Many thanks to all of the bread testers and tasters who helped with these recipes. A special thanks to Laura Jane Wright for all of her input and help; and also to my husband, Lee, and daughters, Rachel and Katie, for all of their encouragement and help.

CONTENTS

INTRODUCTION

Shortly after purchasing an automated bread machine, I became frustrated by the lack of bread machine recipes. When other owners were queried, although excited about the machines, nearly everyone was dissatisfied with available recipes and, consequently, attempting to adapt recipes to their machines.

After months of testing and tasting, this cookbook is a compilation of many wonderful and different bread recipes possible using any bread machine.

If you are unfamiliar with the automated bread machines, you are in for a treat. These machines have removable pans into which you place your ingredients, insert the pan, push a button and then remove your baked homemade bread when completed, about 4 hours (give or take) later. It is that easy. If you enjoy the process of kneading the dough yourself, you may select a cycle to knead the dough the first time, let it rise once and tell you when it's ready to come out of the machine for you to complete the process. That is truly the best of both worlds.

If you are looking at various machines and are unsure about whether it is a worthwhile purchase — it is. If you feel you won't eat enough bread to justify the purchase, you probably would increase your bread consumption — fresh, homemade bread just does not compare to "store bought." You may also make small, mini loaves every day or every other day so that your bread is always fresh.

Some people are concerned about weight gain due to eating more bread if they purchase a machine. When you make your own bread, you control the amount of sugar and fats in the bread. Many of the recipes in this book are relatively low in calories.

Each of the various machines is slightly unique. For example, some machines bake round loaves and others, rectangular. One machine may have a special compartment for the placement of yeast. One may require liquid ingredients first and another, last. Please see *Comparisons of Automated Bread Machines*, page 3, for specific information on each machine and hints for using them.

Hopefully the information in *Bread Ingredients*, page 12, will give you enough information and confidence to try adapting your own recipes to your machine — or to try making up your own.

One of the best features of having an automated bread machine is that you control what goes into your bread — with no more than 5 minutes of your time. Experiment — if you have a favorite cereal, use it in bread. Likewise, if you eat jam on all of your bread, try baking it right into the bread! Be bold and have fun with your breads and machine!

COMPARISONS OF AUTOMATED BREAD MACHINES

If shopping for an automated bread machine, it is helpful to compare the various features of each model. For this comparison, information was gathered from the operating and recipe manuals provided with the machines, representatives of the various manufacturing firms, machine owners and testing. The information gathered from this comparison has been compiled into the following table and remarks.

	DAK	Hitachi	Matsushita (Panasonic National)	Maxim	Regal	Sanyo	Welbilt	Zojir-ushi
ONE LOAF								
cups of flour	3-4	2, 3	2, 3	2	2.5, 3.5	2	2, 3	3-4
loaf size (lb)	1.5+	1, 1.5	1, 1.5	1	1, 1.5+	1	1, 1.5	1.5+
loaf shape:								
round	x						x	
rectangular		x	x	x	x	x		x
Cycles:								
white bread	x	x	x	x	x	x	x	x
French bread	x	-	- x	x	-	-	x	x
sweet bread	x	-	-	-	-	-	x	-
raisin bread	x	x	-	-	x	x	x	x
rapid rise	-	x	- x	x	x	-	-	x
quick bread	-	-	- x	-	-	-	-	x
jam making	-	- x	-	-	-	-	-	x

	DAK	Hitachi	Matsushita (Panasonic National)-	Maxim	Regal	Sanyo	Welbilt	Zojir ushi
light/dark	x	x	x	x	- x	-	x	x
timer	x	x	x	x	x	x	x	x
dough cycle	x	x	x	x	x	x	x	x
programmable	-	-	-	-	-	-	-	x
rice maker	-	- x	-	-	-	-	-	-
rye/whole grain	-	-	-	x	-	-	-	-

Timing of cycles (in minutes) on white bread setting:

	DAK	Hitachi	Matsushita	Maxim	Regal	Sanyo	Welbilt	Zojirushi
1st knead	15	7	10-30	20	7	10	20	10
1st rise	60	5	15-45	--	5	5	60	5
2nd knead	18	16-24	45-65	--	16-24	18	22	20-25
rise (& shape)	95	130-140	90-100	145-150	130-140	47-65	95	70
baking	50	53-60	45	40-45	53-60	40-55	50	50-55
cooling	20	20-31	--	--	20-31	--	15	13-38

Hours to completion on White Bread cycle (approximate):

DAK	Hitachi	Matsushita	Maxim	Regal	Sanyo	Welbilt	Zojirushi
4	4	4:15	3:30	4	3	4	3:50

DAK

The Dak is capable of handling more than 3 cups of flour, if using a combination of low gluten flour or flour substitutes along with bread flour. If using the dough cycle only, much more than 3 cups may be used since the second rising occurs in the pan in which it is baked. The bread pan itself is placed into the machine and the kneading hook helps to seal it in place. For this reason, dry ingredients are placed into the pan first. Recipes in this cookbook should be read from the bottom up so that yeast is your first ingredient. I found that the machine shimmies during the kneading cycles. Make sure you have lots of room between the machine and the edge of your counter!

HITACHI

There are several different models with varying capacities. Ingredients may be placed in the machine in any order unless using the timer, in which case wet ingredients should be placed first.

MATSUSHITA (NATIONAL/PANASONIC BREAD BAKERY)

Matsushita sells bread machines under the names of National Bread Bakery or Panasonic Bread Bakery. In addition to the different names, there are different models with varying capacities. French bread cycles are included on machines National SDBT6N and Panasonic SDBT6P. These same machines also have a quick bread setting for baking (although you must first mix the ingredients together) and a cycle which enables you to remove the dough, place a filling in it and return it to the machine for baking. The Panasonic SDBT2P is the only Matsushita machine which does not have the rapid rise cycle. It also does not have the capacity to adjust bread color.

One complaint about these machines is the company's recommendation to place raisins, etc. into the machine at the beginning of the cycle. This results in crushed raisin bread instead of whole raisins or like ingredients. During my testing, however,

I found that these ingredients may be added during the "rise" period immediately following the completion of the first kneading. The ingredients will sit on top of the dough until the second kneading.

These machines have a special dispenser into which the yeast is placed and then dropped into the dough at the proper time. When using the timer cycle, the machine kneads the dough when the machine is turned on and adds the yeast later. This allows you to add the raisins after the kneading and have raisin bread on the timer, unlike any of the other models. As there is no viewing window, the lid may be opened briefly during any process except baking to check on the progress. The loaves are similar in shape to bread purchased in a store.

MAXIM

This machine has a rye bread setting for rye and other whole grains. There is no raisin bread cycle, and you may add raisins with other ingredients at the beginning.

REGAL

Light/dark controls are found on the deluxe model only. When using the deluxe model, wet ingredients must be added first if using the timer; otherwise they may be entered in any order. The information provided in the table on timing of cycles is for the deluxe model only.

SANYO

Sold as a "no frills" machine, the Sanyo offers the basic cycles and completes the bread in three hours.

WELBILT ABM 100

Yeast and then dry ingredients are always placed into the pan first. Recipes in this cookbook should be read from the bottom up. Our testor reported that while tasting great, the tops of some loaves did not brown, collapsed or were uneven. Welbilt has a newsletter which goes to the owners of their machines.

ZOJIRUSHI

This machine has a cake (quick bread) and jam cycle as well as the ability to program your own kneading/rising lengths. All work well and are nice additional features. The machine also has a prekneading, warming cycle to bring all ingredients up to the proper temperature to mix with the yeast. Unlike some other machines, you need not worry about bringing ingredients to room or lukewarm temperature. Although there are no specific cycles for them, this machine also makes sweet and whole grain breads.

PLEASE NOTE: Read the recipe carefully. Do not exceed the capacity for your machine.

All of the recipes in this book were tested on each machine's standard white cycle. This was to maintain consistency among the recipes and the various machines.

HINTS ABOUT USING BREAD MACHINES

Here are some additional hints which may be useful to successful automatic bread baking:

- Some people find it difficult to cut the round loaves into usable sandwich slices. It is suggested that you cut the loaf in half and slice each half. I have found that when not using bread for sandwiches, cutting it into pie shapes works quite well. One owner says she finds the top of the loaf is not always baked sufficiently or that it collapses; if that is the case, use a smaller size recipe.

- Always place your ingredients into the pan in such a way that the yeast is not touching the liquid. This is especially imperative when using a timer cycle.

- Many of the machines recommend bringing ingredients to lukewarm or room temperature prior to placing in the machine. Sourdough starter would be included in this group.

- Butter or margarine may simply be cut into quarters for placing in the machines.

- I find using egg substitutes is the easiest for recipes calling for fractions of eggs. One egg equivalent is ¼ cup; therefore, half an egg equals 2 tablespoons.

- Always place any dry milk next to the yeast, farthest from the liquids.

- Breads containing all bread or white flour will be higher rising than those containing whole wheat or other darker flours. Be sure not to use too large a recipe size to avoid overflowing your pan or having the top portion remain uncooked.

- Make sure that you remove and clean the kneading rod or paddle from the pan after each use. If the rod is "frozen," run warm water into the pan and let sit for a few minutes. If it still does not come out, hold the rod in one hand and the bottom section which makes it turn in the other — twist in opposite directions. If you continually have a problem with this, try putting a very small amount of oil on the rod before inserting it.

- Humidity will add moisture to dough. Add an extra tablespoon or two of flour should the consistency not look right.

- For altitudes over 3,000 feet, you may find it necessary to adjust recipes as follows: decrease yeast amount by approximately ½ teaspoon. Decrease sugar a little.

- Recipes in this cookbook are given in 3 sizes. Choose whichever size is desired or appropriate for your machine's capacity.

- Unless making a sourdough, milk should not sit for more than 1 or 2 hours on a timer cycle. Eggs should not be used at all on a timer; use powdered eggs if needed.

- Occasionally, you may have some leftover bread and wonder what to do with it, aside from feeding ducks, of course! Lots of recipes call for bread crumbs or other bread by-products which are easily made at home and are a great way to use those leftovers. Slice leftover bread and place on baking sheet. Dry out in 140°- 250° oven for several hours — until just a hint of color shows.

  Melba Toast: slices should be very thin.
  Zwieback: slices should be thick and well dried.
  Croutons: cube dried bread in a blender or food processor.
    Store in a tightly closed container.
  Bread Crumbs: as with croutons, put bread in blender or
    processor and grind until finely ground. Use those leftover
    spicy breads such as herb, oregano or dill to make croutons
    or crumbs — great in salads or as breading for fish or chicken.

- When trying to adapt some of your recipes to fit your machines, you may run into a few problems. Listed below are problems I have found and solutions.

Dough rises too high, then collapses — Dough rose too long or pan is too small. Try cutting back the recipe.

Loaf has a strong yeast flavor — Too much yeast was used.

Loaf rises too high — Not enough salt, too much sugar and/or yeast.

Loaf does not rise — Flour type is low in gluten, resulting in a small, dense loaf; or too much salt; or not enough sugar or yeast.

Loaf has very uneven top — Not enough liquid.

Pale in color — Not enough sugar.

Last but not least, don't ruin your great, homemade bread by not storing it properly. Allow the bread to cool completely prior to wrapping it in plastic or aluminum foil and keep wrapped bread in a cool, dry location.

BREAD INGREDIENTS

Yeast

A living plant, yeast eats sugar and produces carbon dioxide which, in turn, mixes with gluten in flour to make the dough rise. Simply stated, without yeast your bread will be a flat, unleavened bread. Regular active dry yeast may be purchased packaged in individual envelopes or in bulk, found normally in the baking section of any grocery store. Compressed yeast, packaged as cakes, may be found in the refrigerated section of grocery stores. In addition, you may use a fast-rising yeast such as FLEISCHMANN'S RapidRise™, also packaged in individual envelopes, for a faster rise. There may be a special cycle on your machine for this type of yeast.

One package of yeast equals approximately 2½ teaspoons or a scant tablespoon. If you use a portion of an envelope of yeast, Fleischmann's recommends that you reseal the package tightly and store it in the freezer or refrigerator. If you purchase yeast in bulk, store it in an airtight container in the refrigerator. Yeast should be brought to room temperature prior to use and should be used prior to the expiration date. In experimenting with recipes, I have found no significant difference between using a teaspoon, half package or whole package of yeast regardless of the size of the loaf made. Some machine owners, however, report that a full package of yeast is too much. For that reason, specific yeast amounts are provided in the recipes as a guideline.

Liquids

Liquids provide the yeast the initial capacity to grow. In conventional bread baking, the liquid is heated to lukewarm and the yeast is "proofed," activating the yeast. Milk gives the bread a soft, thin texture while water makes it crusty. Other liquids which may be used include vegetable water (water in which vegetables have been cooked), fruit juices, sour cream, yogurt, cottage or ricotta cheese, coffee, tea, soups, beer or even diluted liqueurs. In many of my recipes, I use nonfat dry milk or a buttermilk powder. Both give the desired texture of either the milk or buttermilk and are convenient to use. They may be found in any grocery store. Liquids used in the automated bread machines need not be heated to lukewarm prior to being placed in the pan; it is recommended, however, that liquids be at room temperature.

Fats

In bread baking, fats provide flavor, make the bread moist and give it a soft crumb. Fats used interchangeably include margarine, butter, vegetable oil of any kind, shortening or lard. Some recipes specify olive oil as it imparts a distinctive taste; however, you may use any vegetable oil. Unlike conventional bread baking, butter or margarine need not be melted to be placed in the machine.

Sugar

A necessity in yeast bread baking, sugar feeds the yeast, enabling it to rise. In addition, it assists in the browning of the crust. Sugar substitutes for bread baking purposes include white or brown sugar, barley malt syrup, honey, molasses, maple syrup, and even jam, jellies or marmalades. Sugar substitutes used for diet purposes, such as NutraSweet™, etc. should not be used since they break down during the heating process. Interestingly enough, honey is a natural preservative for your breads.

Salt

A growth-inhibitor of the yeast, salt provides a counter-balance for the sugar. It also brings out the flavor of the bread.

Eggs

A nonessential ingredient, eggs are sometimes used in bread baking to add rich-ness, color and flavor. Egg substitutes may be used interchangeably for eggs. In fact, in cases where half eggs are used, I find it easier to use the substitutes. Egg powder is also available which is useful in recipes which require eggs when the timer cycle is used. This may be difficult to locate, but may be found in a health food store or ordered by mail (see Source Guide, page 163). If dieting and/or concerned about cholesterol levels, substitute 1 whole egg and 1 egg white for 2 eggs required in recipes.

Flour

There are many different kinds of flours, grains or cereals which may be used for structure in your bread baking. As a general rule, white or bread flour should be at least 50 percent of the flour or grain used. A higher percentage will result in a low, heavy density bread. With this "rule" in mind, flours may be substituted cup for cup with other flours, grains or cereals. A detailed description of various grains and flours follows.

Prior to explaining the various flours and flour substitutes, some background information may be helpful. Any grain which has not yet had the hull, or outer lining, removed is called a groat. You will usually hear oats and buckwheat referred to in this way. Once the hulls are removed, the remaining kernel contains the bran, germ and endosperm. The bran and germ of any grain contain the majority of the nutrients. Up to 80 percent of the vitamins and minerals are lost by the grinding and refining of the grain into white flour (which consists of pure endosperm). A general rule of thumb is that the darker the flour (whether it is wheat, rye, rice, etc.), the more of the germ and bran are included and, hence, the more nutritional the bread. Any flour containing the germ and/or bran should be refrigerated for maximum freshness; at the very least, these flours should be stored in a dark, cool place.

While making yeast breads, you normally use a wheat flour base which, when kneaded, develops gluten. The gluten forms an elastic substance which traps the carbon dioxide released from the yeast. This is the key ingredient in the wheat which makes the dough rise. Other flours with less gluten must be mixed with wheat flour to a maximum ratio of 1 to 1. The higher the non- or low-gluten flour amount, the smaller and denser in texture your bread will be.

WHEAT

Wheat Flours: The most common flour for bread baking is that obtained from wheat. One walk down the flour aisle of your local grocery store will tell you that there are several different kinds of wheat flours. Differences come from where the wheat is grown, making it hard or soft, what section of the wheat kernel is used, or how the flour is milled and what treatments are provided after the milling.

All Purpose Flour: A blend of hard and soft wheats that may be used for a variety of baking needs including breads and cakes. All purpose loses many of its natural vitamins and nutrients during the milling process. Hence, it is usually "enriched" by replacing 4 of those nutrients: iron, thiamine, riboflavin and niacin. Bleached all purpose flour is chemically whitened while unbleached flour is allowed to whiten naturally.

Bread Flour: The recommended flour for most of the recipes in this book. It is derived from hard wheat, meaning it is higher both in protein and gluten. You will find that bread flour will give you a finer grain bread. You may also hear this bread referred to as *bromated*, which is a dough conditioner used to enhance the gluten's development. If your grocery store does not carry bread flour, do not hesitate to request the management to add it to their inventory. Bread flour is made by both Pillsbury and Gold Medal as well as many smaller mills, some of which sell via catalogs (see Source Guide, page163).

Whole Wheat Flour: Milled from the entire wheat kernel, it is light brown in color and contains all the natural nutrients. A healthy addition to bread, it is lower in gluten than the white flours and should not exceed 50 percent of the flour ingredients. You may also see this referred to as graham flour and sold in health food stores. Some mills label their graham flour differently than their whole wheat as the graham contains 100 percent of the kernel while the whole wheat may have had some minor cleaning and sifting. Every mill is different in their labeling, hence for our purposes, I call both whole wheat.

Gluten Flour/Gluten: The gluten protein is removed from wheat flour by rinsing off the starch. This is then dried and ground to be added to regular white flour. Pure gluten is slightly gray in color but does not affect the color of your bread. It may be purchased through a well stocked health food store or by mail-order (see Source Guide, page 163). This is added in small amounts to your dry ingredients in low-gluten bread dough for a lighter texture.

Wheat Germ: One of the best parts of the wheat kernel, the germ is the embryo of the wheat berry. A wonderful source of protein, fat, vitamins and minerals, wheat germ can be added to all baked goods by placing 1 tablespoon in the bottom of your measuring cup prior to filling with flour. It gives breads a slightly nutty flavoring. Opened jars of wheat germ must be refrigerated.

Wheat Berry: Very high in protein and low in calories, this is the original form of the wheat grain before any grinding or milling. The berries must be soaked, preferably overnight, prior to use. They are the most common sprouted berry used for "sprout" bread. The berries may be bought in health food stores or ordered by mail (see Sources Guide, page 163). Keep in a dry, cool place.

Cracked Wheat: Crushed, toasted wheat berries. Cracked wheat must be soaked a minimum of 1 hour prior to kneading. I always soak the cracked wheat right in the liquid of the dough mixture.

Wheat Bulgur: Parboiled, crushed and toasted wheat berries — sometimes used interchangeably with cracked wheat.

Rolled Wheat Flakes: Similar to rolled oats, wheat flakes are available as a cereal at a health food store. They add a unique flavor and texture to bread.

BARLEY

Barley: Barley flour will only be found in health food stores. It has a very low gluten content and must be used in conjunction with a high gluten flour. Barley has a mild nutty flavor. Generally, barley flour is a low percentage of all flour used in bread recipes.

Barley Malt: A heavy syrup used in both bread baking and beer making, barley malt gives bread a rich, grainy flavor. Pure barley malt tastes similar to blackstrap molasses and the two may be used interchangeably. It is wonderful when used with seeds such as caraway, anise or fennel. The malt itself is made by soaking the whole barley grains, sprouting them, drying and grinding them. Available in a health food or beer making store.

CORN

Cornmeal: Ground from corn kernels, cornmeal is found in any grocery store. Most commonly used is the yellow variety, but try also the white cornmeal which is milled from white corn. Corn is less nutritious by itself than many of its grain cousins.

Blue Corn: Used for both cornmeal and flour, blue corn is attributed to the Hopi Indians of the American Southwest. Blue cornmeal or flour may be used in place of any cornmeal. Blue corn is more nutritious than the yellow or white and has a subtle, sweet taste.

OATS

Rolled Oats: The grinding of oats leaves the bran and germ intact and, therefore, the nutrients. Reasonably high in protein, oats are also high in vitamins B and E. Rolled oats are the most familiar form of oats to most of us. The oat grains are steamed, rolled into flakes and dried.

Oat Bran: In addition to lowering blood cholesterol levels, oat bran is nutritious and adds fiber to a diet. In baking of breads, oat bran will add a nice moisture to the texture.

Oat Flour: Milled or ground rolled oats. Try making your own in your food processor or blender; blend 1 cup at a time at high speed until a fine flour forms — about 1 minute. It is also available for purchase in health food stores or by mail order.

RICE

Rice Grains: Rice is no stranger to most of our dinner tables in the form of boiled grains. The most common grains found in grocery stores have had their hulls removed, hence most of their nutritional value.

Rice Flour: A low gluten flour, this must be used in conjunction with a white flour such as bread flour. You may find this in the Oriental section of your grocery store or in a health food store.

Rice Bran: This has recently been discovered to have the same qualities as oat bran in lowering blood cholesterol levels. As with all bran, it is the outer layer of the kernel and has high nutritional value.

Rice Syrup: A sweetener containing no fructose or sucrose. Syrup may be found in a health food store.

RYE

Rye Flour: Milled from the rye berry or the entire kernel, rye flour has a high nutrient content. The darker the color, the stronger the taste and the nutrient value. There is no gluten in rye flours; this must be used in combination with a white flour. The larger the percentage of rye, the smaller and denser the loaf will be.

Rye Meal: A coarser grind than flour of the rye kernel.

Rye Berry: The berry or kernel of rye, as wheat berries, may be sprouted and used in its entirety in bread for the highest nutritional content.

SOY

Soybeans: A very inexpensive source of high protein, soybeans are used in many different ways and foods.

Soy Flakes: Pressed soybeans which can be added to bread for crunchy, tasty bread.

Soy Flour: High in protein and low in calories, soy flour is often added to high protein, diet type breads. It adds moisture and is a natural preservative. Soy flour is usually added in small amounts as the taste may be found to be somewhat overpowering.

LESSER KNOWN GRAINS

Amaranth: Attributed to the Aztec Indians, amaranth is extremely high in protein, vitamins, minerals and calcium. You can find amaranth grain, cereals, etc., in your health food store and may find some in large grocery stores. The grains themselves may be cooked for a hot cereal, sprouted for salads or breads, toasted as nuts or even popped like popcorn. If you pop it, keep in mind that it may burn easily without oil, but that you shouldn't use too much oil, either.

The history of amaranth is fascinating. When the Aztecs were conquered by the Spaniards, it was discovered that the Aztecs were mixing sacrificial blood with amaranth. In an attempt to end this practice, Cortez ordered all amaranth destroyed. It was during an archeological expedition that some seeds were discovered and later replanted, giving us amaranth once again.

Buckwheat/Kasha: Has a very high protein count. It can be found in cereal form in many grocery and health food stores. Nutritionally, it is rich in vitamins B and E as well as having a high calcium content. Buckwheat flour is most commonly known for its use in pancakes.

Quinoa (pronounced KEEN-wah): A fondly remembered grain from time I spent in Peru. Recently available in the United States, this grain is quickly catching on even though it is somewhat expensive. Extremely high in protein, (anywhere from 14 to 19 percent), quinoa is also an excellent source of calcium, and has a high lysine content, as well as vitamin C, thiamine, riboflavin and niacin. Quinoa grains may be cooked the same as rice. The flour is expensive but worth it in quinoa bread, which has a slightly nutty taste.

It also has an interesting history; Pizzaro attempted to destroy much of the crop in an effort to weaken the Incas during the conquering process. As time passed, the Spaniards looked down upon quinoa as a grain for "heathens" and discounted the nutritional values. To this day, many upper-class Peruvians consider quinoa a grain suitable for the indigenous only!

WHITE AND CHEESE BREADS

WHITE BREAD

This is a very rich bread — terrific for sandwiches. You'll find yourself going back for more and more. It is not, however, one of the more dietetic. Well worth the calories anyway!

	Small	Medium	Large
water	½ cup	⅔ cup	1 cup
margarine/butter	2 tbs.	2½ tbs.	¼ cup
egg	½	⅔	1
sugar	1 tbs.	1⅓ tbs.	2 tbs.
salt	½ tsp.	⅔ tsp.	1 tsp.
bread flour	1½ cup	2 cups	3 cups
nonfat dry milk	2 tbs.	2½ tbs.	¼ cup
yeast	1 tsp.	1½ tsp.	2½ tsp.

SALLY LUNN

A very rich, European tasting bread. The eggs give it lots of terrific taste and color. Tradition says that a young Englishwoman, Sally Lunn, sold this bread on the streets of Bath. Most bread cookbooks contain a version of this, which attests to its wonderful flavor. This is one of those breads which will never last to see leftovers.

	Small	Medium	Large
milk	2 tbs.	2½ tbs.	¼ cup
water	¼ cup	⅓ cup	½ cup
margarine/butter	3½ tbs.	4½ tbs.	7 tbs.
eggs	1½	2	3
salt	¾ tsp.	1 tsp.	1½ tsp.
sugar	2 tbs.	2½ tbs.	¼ cup
bread flour	1½ cups	2 cups	3 cups
yeast	½ tsp.	¾ tsp.	2 tsp.

Note that this is a very high rising loaf. Use less yeast than normal and do not decrease salt amount.

PORTUGUESE SWEET BREAD

Maria and Manuel, from Portugal, are living here while Manuel completes his doctoral degree. She has experimented with recipes to closely resemble those of her country. This is one of my favorites.

	Small	Medium	Large
milk	½ cup	⅔ cup	1 cup
eggs	1	1⅓	2
margarine/butter	1 tbs.	1⅓ tbs.	2 tbs.
sugar	2¼ tbs.	3 tbs.	⅓ cup
salt	⅓ tsp.	½ tsp.	¾ tsp.
bread flour	1½ cups	2 cups	3 cups
yeast	1 tsp.	1½ tsp.	2½ tsp.

Variation: Should you prefer this even sweeter, increase sugar to:

	Small	Medium	Large
	3 tbs.	⅓ cup	½ cup

PORTUGUESE WHITE BREAD

A very light, airy bread. Slightly difficult to cut while hot — but who can wait that long anyway?

	Small	Medium	Large
water	2/3 cup	1 cup	1 1/3 cups
margarine/butter	2 tbs.	3 tbs.	1/4 cup
sugar	2 tsp.	1 tbs.	1 1/3 tbs.
salt	1 tsp.	1 1/2 tsp.	2 tsp.
bread flour	1 7/8 cups	2 3/4 cups	3 2/3 cups
yeast	1 tsp.	1 1/2 tsp.	2 1/2 tsp.

ENGLISH MUFFIN BREAD

This is a really good, easy way to get that English Muffin taste and texture. Great bread to have set on the timer for a hot breakfast bread. In order to have the proper texture, there will be a sunken top to this bread.

	Small	Medium	Large
water	2/3 cup-1 tbs.	1 cup-1½ tbs.	1¼ cups
sugar	1 tsp.	1¼ tsp.	2 tsp.
salt	½ tsp.	2/3 tsp.	1 tsp.
baking soda	dash	⅛ tsp.	¼ tsp.
bread flour	1½ cups	2 cups	3 cups
nonfat dry milk	1½ tbs.	2 tbs.	3 tbs.
yeast	1 tsp.	1½ tsp.	2 tsp.

PEASANT BREAD

This recipe is based on one given to me by Carmen, a friend and neighbor. It's a very moist, chewy bread with a light, crispy crust. Absolutely wonderful with butter or cheese. It is somewhat similar to an English Muffin loaf but more moist.

	Small	Medium	Large
water	¾ cup	1 cup	1½ cups
sugar	1 tsp.	1¼ tsp.	2 tsp.
salt	¾ tsp.	1 tsp.	1½ tsp.
bread flour	1½ cups	2 cups	3 cups
yeast	1 tsp.	1½ tsp.	2 tsp.

SOUR CREAM BREAD

Great sandwich bread. A nice texture and great taste.

	Small	Medium	Large
water	1¼ tbs.	2 tbs.	2½ tbs.
sour cream	⅔ cup	1 cup	1⅓ cups
salt	⅓ tsp.	½ tsp.	⅔ tsp.
baking soda	dash	⅛ tsp.	¼ tsp.
sugar	2 tsp.	1 tbs.	1⅓ tbs.
bread flour	1⅔ cups	2½ cups	3⅓ cups
yeast	1 tsp.	1½ tsp.	2½ tsp.

CRUSTY CUBAN BREAD

Very similar to French bread — great with cheese and/or wine.

	Small	Medium	Large
water	2/3 cup	1 cup	1 1/3 cups
sugar	3/4 tsp.	1 tsp.	1 1/2 tsp.
salt	1 1/2 tsp.	2 tsp.	1 tbs.
bread flour	1 1/2 cups	2 cups	3 cups
yeast	1 tsp.	1 1/2 tsp.	2 1/2 tsp.

If you have a French bread or crusty setting, it may be used for this bread, although it is not necessary.

FRENCH HONEY BREAD

Wonderful, slightly sweet French bread with a light, crispy crust.

	Small	Medium	Large
water	½ cup+1 tbs.	¾ cup	1⅛ cups
honey	1½ tsp.	2 tsp.	1 tbs.
olive oil	1½ tsp.	2 tsp.	1 tbs.
salt	½ tsp.	⅔ tsp.	1 tsp.
sugar	½ tsp.	⅔ tsp.	1 tsp.
bread flour	1½ cups	2 cups	3 cups
yeast	1 tsp.	1½ tsp.	2½ tsp.

ITALIAN BREAD

Makes me think of an outdoor cafe in Florence near the Duomo, with a red and white checkered tablecloth and the bread, cheese and wine on the table.

	Small	Medium	Large
water	½ cup	⅔ cup	1 cup
salt	⅔ tsp.	¾ tsp.	1¼ tsp.
sugar	½ tsp.	⅔ tsp.	1 tsp.
bread flour	1½ cups	2 cups	3 cups
yeast	1 tsp.	1½ tsp.	2½ tsp.

AUSTRIAN MALT BREAD

A slight taste of malt gives this an exotic flavor. I found malted milk powder, made by Carnation, in the grocery store, with other dry milk products.

	Small	Medium	Large
water	½ cup	⅔ cup	1 cup
margarine/butter	1 tbs.	1¼ tbs.	2 tbs.
sugar	¾ tbs.	1 tbs.	1½ tbs.
salt	¾ tsp.	1 tsp.	1½ tsp.
bread flour	1½ cups	2 cups	3 cups
malted milk powder	1½ tbs.	2 tbs.	3 tbs.
yeast	1 tsp.	1½ tsp.	2½ tsp.

BUTTERMILK BREAD

Great taste and texture, a light fluffy bread. If you have some buttermilk in the refrigerator, use it in place of the water and omit the dry powder. Either way, it is equally delicious.

	Small	Medium	Large
water	½ cup	⅔ cup	1 cup
margarine/butter	1 tbs.	1¼ tbs.	2 tbs.
sugar	½ tsp.	⅔ tsp.	1 tsp.
salt	½ tsp.	⅔ tsp.	1 tsp.
bread flour	1½ cups	2 cups	3 cups
buttermilk powder	2 tbs.	2½ tbs.	¼ cup
yeast	1 tsp.	1½ tsp.	2½ tsp.

COTTAGE CHEESE BREAD

A rich sandwich bread. A favorite of my husband.

	Small	Medium	Large
water	2 tbs.	2½ tbs.	¼ cup
cottage cheese	½ cup	⅔ cup	1 cup
margarine/butter	1 tbs.	1¼ tbs.	2 tbs.
egg	½	⅔	1
sugar	1½ tsp.	2 tsp.	1 tbs.
baking soda	dash	⅛ tsp.	¼ tsp.
salt	½ tsp.	⅔ tsp.	1 tsp.
bread flour	1½ cups	2 cups	3 cups
yeast	1 tsp.	1½ tsp.	2½ tsp.

RICOTTA BREAD

This made a huge hit with friends and tasters who ranked it one of the best. Slices very well.

	Small	Medium	Large
milk	3 tbs.	⅓ cup	6 tbs.
ricotta cheese	⅔ cup	1 cup	1⅓ cups
margarine/butter	1¼ tbs.	2 tbs.	2½ tbs.
eggs	½	1	1½
sugar	2 tbs.	2½ tbs.	¼ cup
salt	⅔ tsp.	1 tsp.	1⅓ tsp.
bread flour	1½ cups	2¼ cups	3 cups
yeast	1 tsp.	1½ tsp.	2½ tsp.

CREAM CHEESE BREAD

More of a dessert bread or cake — delicious. Try adding, on the raisin setting, items such as chocolate chips, nuts, raisins or other dried fruits.

	Small	Medium	Large
milk	2 tbs.	3 tbs.	⅓ cup
cream cheese	½ cup	⅔ cup	1 cup
margarine/butter	2 tbs.	2½ tbs.	¼ cup
egg	½	⅔	1
sugar	1½ tbs.	2 tbs.	3 tbs.
salt	½ tsp.	⅔ tsp.	1 tsp.
bread flour	1½ cup	2 cups	3 cups
yeast	1 tsp.	1½ tsp.	2½ tsp.

CHEDDAR CHEESE BREAD

This is a delicious bread. While it may be made on the regular, white bread setting, if made on the raisin bread setting, the cheese is more visible and it has a little better texture. Add diced scallions for a delicious variation.

	Small	Medium	Large
water or milk	½ cup	⅔ cup	1 cup
margarine/butter	1½ tsp.	2 tsp.	1 tbs.
sugar	1½ tsp.	2 tsp.	1 tbs.
salt	¼ tsp.	⅓ tsp.	½ tsp.
bread flour	1½ cups	2 cups	3 cups
yeast	1 tsp.	1½ tsp.	2½ tsp.

at beep add: (If National/Panasonic, add following first kneading)

shredded cheddar			
cheese	⅓ cup+1 tbs.	½ cup	¾ cup
diced scallions,			
optional	⅓ cup+1 tbs.	½ cup	¾ cup

WHOLE WHEAT, GRAIN AND CEREAL BREADS

WHOLE WHEAT I

This is my favorite whole wheat. Slices very well.

	Small	Medium	Large
water	2⁄3 cup	1 cup	1 1⁄3 cups
margarine/butter	2 1⁄2 tbs.	1⁄4 cup	5 tbs.
egg, optional	1⁄2	1	1 1⁄2
sugar	1 1⁄4 tbs.	2 tbs.	2 1⁄2 tbs.
salt	1 tsp.	1 1⁄2 tsp.	2 tsp.
bread flour	1 1⁄3 cups	2 cups	2 2⁄3 cups
whole wheat flour	2⁄3 cup	1 cup	1 1⁄3 cups
nonfat dry milk	2 1⁄2 tbs.	1⁄4 cup	5 tbs.
yeast	1 tsp.	1 1⁄2 tsp.	2 1⁄2 tsp.

WHOLE WHEAT II

A subtle, different whole wheat. The yogurt gives it a great flavor. I have always enjoyed oats with whole wheat.

	Small	Medium	Large
plain nonfat yogurt	2/3 cup	1 cup	1 1/3 cups
water	2 1/2 tbs.	1/4 cups	5 tbs.
margarine/butter	1 1/4 tbs.	2 tbs.	2 1/2 tbs.
sugar	1 1/3 tbs.	2 tbs.	2 2/3 tbs.
salt	1 tsp.	1 1/2 tsp.	2 tsp.
bread flour	1 cup	1 1/2 cups	2 cups
oats	1/3 cup	1/2 cup	2/3 cup
whole wheat flour	2/3 cup	1 cup	1 1/3 cups
yeast	1 tsp.	1 1/2 tsp.	2 1/2 tsp.

WHOLE WHEAT III

This is a very good, lowfat bread.

	Small	**Medium**	**Large**
water	2/3 cup	1 cup	1 1/3 cups
margarine/butter	1 tbs.	1 1/2 tbs.	2 tbs.
sugar	1 tbs.	1 1/2 tbs.	2 tbs.
salt	1/2 tsp.	3/4 tsp.	1 tsp.
whole wheat flour	1 cup	1 1/2 cups	2 cups
bread flour	1 cup	1 1/2 cups	2 cups
nonfat dry milk	2 1/2 tbs.	3 1/2 tbs.	5 tbs.
yeast	1 tsp.	1 1/2 tsp.	2 1/2 tsp.

SPROUT BREAD

This is superb. Worth the trouble of sprouting the berries, (which is actually quite fun — especially with children helping). The wheat berries are so good for you, too!

	Small	Medium	Large
water	½ cup	¾ cup	1 cup
margarine/butter	1¼ tbs.	2 tbs.	2½ tbs.
sugar	2 tsp.	1 tbs.	1⅓ tbs.
salt	1 tsp.	1½ tsp.	2 tsp.
sprouted wheat berries	⅓ cup	½ cup	⅔ cup
bread flour	1⅔ cups	2½ cups	3⅓ cups
nonfat dry milk	2 tbs.	3 tbs.	¼ cup
yeast	1 tsp.	1½ tsp.	2½ tsp.

Two to three days prior to making this bread, place ⅓ - ½ cup wheat berries in a sprouting jar (or any glass jar with cheesecloth tied down with a rubber band). Cover with water and allow to sit overnight (at least 12 hours). Drain and rinse again, right through the screen or cheesecloth, and set the jar mouth side down at a 45° angle in a warm, dark place. Rinse sprouts twice a day. They are ready for use when you see small sprouts of about ⅛ to ¼ inch. (Wheat berry sprouts should be no longer than the berry itself.)

NINE-GRAIN BREAD

Nine-grain cereal consists of cracked wheat, barley, corn, millet, oats, triticale, brown rice, soya and flax seed and is available for purchase either in bulk or pre-boxed. May be carried in a large grocery store or a natural food store. Seven-grain cereal may be used as a substitute. Some stores carry one and not the other. Another "must try."

	Small	Medium	Large
water	2/3 cup	1 cup	1 1/3 cups
margarine/butter	1 1/4 tbs.	2 tbs.	2 1/2 tbs.
brown sugar	1 tbs.	1 1/2 tbs.	2 tbs.
salt	2/3 tsp.	1 tsp.	1 1/3 tsp.
9-grain cereal	2/3 cup	1 cup	1 1/3 cup
bread flour	1 1/3 cups	2 cups	2 2/3 cups
nonfat dry milk	2 tbs.	3 tbs.	1/4 cup
yeast	1 tsp.	1 1/2 tsp.	2 1/2 tsp.

CRACKED WHEAT BREAD

One of the best. A natural, great tasting bread with a bit of crunchiness. Both the cracked wheat and gluten are available at a local health food store.

	Small	Medium	Large
water	1 cup-1½ tbs.	1¼ cups	1⅔ cups
cracked wheat	⅓ cup	½ cup	⅔ cup
vegetable oil	1¼ tbs.	2 tbs.	2½ tbs.
honey	⅔ tbs.	1 tbs.	1⅓ tbs.
salt	⅔ tsp.	1 tsp.	1⅓ tsp.
gluten, optional	1⅓ tbs.	2 tbs.	2⅔ tbs.
whole wheat flour	⅔ cup	1 cup	1⅓ cups
bread flour	1 cup	1½ cups	2 cups
yeast	2½ tsp.	2½ tsp.	2½ tsp.

Allow the cracked wheat to sit in liquid at least one hour.

HIGH PROTEIN DIET/CORNELL BREAD

Much better than the store bought diet breads which use "sawdust fiber" as filler. This is a tasty, dense loaf. Makes good sandwiches. The recipe is based on a formula devised for superior nutrition in bread by faculty at Cornell University. Wheat germ, soy flour and nonfat dry milk are added to each cup of flour in the Cornell Formula, this recipe makes it easier.

	Small	Medium	Large
water	⅔ cup	1 cup	1⅓ cups
vegetable oil	2 tsp.	1 tbs.	1⅓ tbs.
honey	2 tsp.	1 tbs.	1⅓ tbs.
salt	½ tsp.	¾ tsp.	1 tsp.
wheat germ	1⅓ tbs.	2 tbs.	2⅔ tbs.
soy flour	2½ tbs.	¼ cup	5 tbs.
whole wheat flour	⅔ cup	1 cup	1⅓ cups
bread flour	1 cup-1½ tbs.	1¼ cups	1⅔ cups
nonfat dry milk	2½ tbs.	¼ cup	5 tbs.
yeast	1 tsp.	1½ tsp.	2½ tsp.

BRAN I

A wonderfully hearty bread and so healthy. Wheat bran is also known as Millers Bran, and like oat bran, can be found in health food stores.

	Small	Medium	Large
water	2⁄3 cup	1 cup	1 1⁄3 cups
margarine/butter	1 1⁄4 tbs.	2 tbs.	2 1⁄2 tbs.
brown sugar	2 tsp.	1 tbs.	1 1⁄3 tbs.
salt	2⁄3 tsp.	1 tsp.	1 1⁄3 tsp.
wheat germ	2 1⁄2 tbs.	1⁄4 cup	5 tbs.
whole wheat flour	1⁄3 cup	1⁄2 cup	2⁄3 cup
oat or wheat bran	2⁄3 cup	1 cup	1 1⁄3 cups
bread flour	1 cup	1 1⁄2 cups	2 cups
yeast	1 tsp.	1 1⁄2 tsp.	2 1⁄2 tsp.

BRAN II

Good tasting, good texture and good for you!.

	Small	Medium	Large
water	2/3 cup	1 cup	1 1/3 cups
margarine/butter	2 tsp.	1 tbs.	1 1/3 tbs.
sugar	2 tsp.	1 tbs.	1 1/3 tbs.
salt	1 tsp.	1 1/2 tsp.	2 tsp.
oat or wheat bran	1/2 cup	3/4 cup	1 cup
bread flour	1 cup+2 1/2 tbs.	1 3/4 cups	2 1/3 cups
yeast	1 tsp.	1 1/2 tsp.	2 1/2 tsp.

MULTI-GRAIN BREAD

A hearty, somewhat dense, full-of-fiber bread that is wonderful with a stew or homemade soup. You can substitute cracked wheat for bulgur.

	Small	Medium	Large
water	1 cup-½ tbs.	1¼ cups	1⅔ cups
vegetable oil	2 tbs.	3 tbs.	¼ cups
honey	1¼ tbs.	2 tbs.	2½ tbs.
salt	1 tsp.	1½ tsp.	2 tsp.
bulgur wheat	2½ tbs.	¼ cup	5 tbs.
wheat germ	1⅓ tbs.	2 tbs.	2⅔ tbs.
wheat or oat bran	⅓ cup	½ cup	⅔ cup
rye flour	⅓ cup	½ cup	⅔ cup
oats	2½ tbs.	¼ cup	5 tbs.
gluten, optional	1 tbs.	1½ tbs.	2 tbs.
bread flour	1 cup	1½ cups	2¼ cups
nonfat dry milk	2½ tbs.	¼ cup	5 tbs.
yeast	1 tsp.	1½ tsp.	2½ tsp.

WHEAT FLAKE BREAD

Great bread — the wheat flakes, similar to oat flakes, give it a nice texture along with being nutritious.

	Small	Medium	Large
water	2/3 cup	1 cup	1 1/3 cups
margarine/butter	1 1/4 tbs.	2 tbs.	2 1/2 tbs.
brown sugar	2 tsp.	1 tbs.	1 1/3 tbs.
salt	1/3 tsp.	1/2 tsp.	2/3 tsp.
gluten, optional	2/3 tbs.	1 tbs.	1 1/3 tbs.
rolled wheat flakes	1/3 cup	1/2 cup	2/3 cup
whole wheat flour	2/3 cup	1 cup	1 1/3 cups
bread flour	1 cup	1 1/2 cups	2 cups
nonfat dry milk	2 tbs.	3 tbs.	1/4 cup
yeast	1 tsp.	1 1/2 tsp.	2 1/2 tsp.

WHEAT GERM SESAME BREAD

This is an absolutely wonderful, light, airy bread.

	Small	Medium	Large
water	2/3 cup	1 cup	1 1/3 cups
vegetable oil	2 tbs.	3 tbs.	1/4 cup
honey	2 tbs.	3 tbs.	1/4 cup
eggs	1/2	1	1 1/2
salt	2/3 tsp.	1 tsp.	1 1/3 tsp.
wheat germ	2 tbs.	3 tbs.	1/4 cup
sesame seeds	1 tbs.	1 1/2 tbs.	2 tbs.
whole wheat flour	2/3 cup	1 cup	1 1/3 cup
bread flour	1 1/3 cups	2 cups	2 2/3 cups
yeast	1 tsp.	1 1/2 tsp.	2 1/2 tsp.

WHOLE WHEAT OATMEAL BREAD

Great, wholesome bread — slices well. One of my favorites.

	Small	Medium	Large
water	2/3 cup	1 cup	1 1/3 cups
margarine/butter	2 1/2 tbs.	1/4 cup	5 tbs.
eggs	1/2	1	1 1/2
sugar	1 1/3 tbs.	2 tbs.	2 2/3 tbs.
salt	1 1/4 tsp.	2 tsp.	2 1/2 tsp.
bread flour	1 cup	1 1/2 cups	2 cups
whole wheat flour	1/2 cup	3/4 cup	1 cup
oats	1/3 cup	1/2 cup	2/3 cup
wheat germ	2 1/2 tbs.	1/4 cup	5 tbs.
nonfat dry milk	2 1/2 tbs.	1/4 cup	5 tbs.
yeast	1 tsp.	1 1/2 tsp.	2 1/2 tsp.

OATMEAL BREAD

A terrific oatmeal loaf!

	Small	**Medium**	**Large**
water	⅔ cup	1 cup	1⅓ cups
margarine/butter	2½ tbs.	4 tbs.	5 tbs.
sugar	1⅓ tbs.	2 tbs.	2⅔ tbs.
salt	1 tsp.	1½ tsp.	2 tsp.
oats	⅔ cup	1 cup	1⅓ cups
bread flour	1⅓ cups	2 cups	2⅔ cups
buttermilk powder	3 tbs.	⅓ cup	6 tbs.
yeast	1 tsp.	1½ tsp.	2½ tsp.

Variation: CINNAMON OATMEAL BREAD
This wonderful, sweet oatmeal bread is great for breakfast. Add to the recipe:

	Small	Medium	Large
cinnamon	⅓ tsp.	½ tsp.	⅔ tsp.

OAT WHEAT BREAD

This bread, dipped in hot cheese (out of a microwave) is a great appetizer — similar to cheese fondue.

	Small	Medium	Large
water	1 cup-1½ tbs.	1¼ cups	1⅔ cups
margarine/butter	1¼ tbs.	2 tbs.	2½ tbs.
sugar	1⅓ tbs.	2 tbs.	2⅔ tbs.
salt	1 tsp.	1½ tsp.	2 tsp.
bread flour	1 cup	1½ cups	2 cups
oat wheat flour*	1 cup	1½ cups	2 cups
yeast	1 tsp.	1½ tsp.	2½ tsp.

* made by Gold Medal; available in grocery stores.

HONEY NUT OATMEAL BREAD

While many grocery stores carry a honey nut oatmeal bread for sandwiches, this seems more of a dessert-type bread to me. Absolutely delicious and a "must try."

	Small	Medium	Large
water	2/3 cup	1 cup	1 1/3 cups
vegetable oil	1 1/3 tbs.	2 tbs.	2 2/3 tbs.
honey	1 1/3 tbs.	2 tbs.	2 2/3 tbs.
salt	2/3 tsp.	1 tsp.	1 1/3 tsp.
oats	2/3 cup	1 cup	1 1/3 cups
whole wheat flour	1/3 cup	1/2 cup	2/3 cup
bread flour	1 cup	1 1/2 cups	2 cups
nonfat dry milk	2 tbs.	3 tbs.	1/4 cup
yeast	1 tsp.	1 1/2 tsp.	2 1/2 tsp.

At beep add: (If National/Panasonic, add following first kneading)

chopped walnuts	1/3 cup	1/2 cup	2/3 cup

ALMOND OATMEAL BREAD

A wonderful, tasty bread. The light almond taste combined with oats is a delightful combination. A "must try."

	Small	Medium	Large
milk	⅔ cup	1 cup	1⅓ cups
margarine	1¼ tbs.	2 tbs.	2½ tbs.
almond paste	1 tbs.	1½ tbs.	2 tbs.
almond extract	1 tsp.	1½ tsp.	2 tsp.
sugar	1 tsp.	1½ tsp.	2 tsp.
salt	1 tsp.	1½ tsp.	2 tsp.
oats	⅔ cup	1 cup	1⅓ cups
bread flour	1⅓ cups	2 cups	2⅔ cups
yeast	1 tsp.	1½ tsp.	2½ tsp.

At beep add: (If National/Panasonic, add following first kneading)

	Small	Medium	Large
slivered almonds	2½ tbs.	¼ cup	5 tbs.

ALMOND BREAD

Just a hint of almond flavor gives this bread a wonderful, sweet taste.

	Small	Medium	Large
milk	½ cup	⅔ cup	1 cup
margarine/butter	1 tbs.	1⅓ tbs.	2 tbs.
almond paste	2 tbs.	2½ tbs.	¼ cup
salt	½ tsp.	⅔ tsp.	1 tsp.
bread flour	1½ cups	2 cups	3 cups
yeast	1 tsp.	1½ tsp.	2½ tsp.

If desired, during the final rising cycle, sprinkle top with slivered almonds for a decorative finish to the bread.

OAT BREAD

A terrific tasting bread, and so good for you, too.

	Small	**Medium**	**Large**
water	1 cup-1½ tbs.	1¼ cups	1⅓ cups
margarine/butter	1¼ tbs.	2 tbs.	2½ tbs.
sugar	2 tbs.	3 tbs.	¼ cup
gluten, optional	2 tbs.	3 tbs.	¼ cup
salt	½ tsp.	¾ tsp.	1 tsp.
oat bran	⅓ cup	½ cup	⅔ cup
oats	⅓ cup	½ cup	⅔ cup
oat flour	⅓ cup	½ cup	⅔ cup
bread flour	1 cup	1½ cups	2 cups
nonfat dry milk	2 tbs.	3 tbs.	¼ cup
yeast	1 tsp.	1½ tsp.	2½ tsp.

OATMEAL SESAME BREAD

This delicious sweet bread is another good choice for breakfast.

	Small	Medium	Large
water	⅔ cup	1 cup	1⅓ cups
margarine/butter	1 tbs.	1½ tbs.	2 tbs.
brown sugar	1 tbs.	1½ tbs.	2 tbs.
cinnamon, optional	½ tsp.	¾ tsp.	1 tsp.
salt	⅔ tsp.	1 tsp.	1⅓ tsp.
sesame seeds	2½ tbs.	¼ cup	5 tbs.
oats	⅓ cup	½ cup	⅔ cup
whole wheat flour	⅓ cup	½ cup	⅔ cup
bread flour	1⅓ cups	2 cups	2⅔ cups
yeast	1 tsp.	1½ tsp.	2½ tsp.

CREAM OF WHEAT BREAD

You'll have people wondering what your secret ingredient is. This slices extremely well and makes excellent French toast.

	Small	Medium	Large
milk	2/3 cup	1 cup	1 1/3 cups
margarine/butter	2 1/2 tbs.	1/4 cup	5 tbs.
eggs	1/2	1	1 1/2
sugar	1 1/3 tbs.	2 tbs.	2 2/3 tbs.
salt	1 1/4 tsp.	2 tsp.	2 1/2 tsp.
gluten, optional	1 tbs.	1 1/2 tbs.	2 tbs.
bread flour	1 1/3 cups	2 cups	2 2/3 cups
cream of wheat*	2/3 cup	1 cup	1 1/3 cups
yeast	1 tsp.	1 1/2 tsp.	2 1/2 tsp.

* uncooked

SHREDDED WHEAT BREAD

This is a very tasty, different bread. If you have another favorite cereal, try it in place of the shredded wheat. A great way to use up the end of the box!

	Small	**Medium**	**Large**
water	1 cup-1½ tbs.	1¼ cups	1⅔ cups
vegetable oil	1⅓ tbs.	2 tbs.	2⅔ tbs.
honey	⅔ tbs.	1 tbs.	1⅓ tbs.
salt	⅔ tsp.	1 tsp.	1⅓ tsp.
shredded wheat	⅓ cup	½ cup	⅔ cup
bread flour	1½ cups	2¼ cups	3 cups
nonfat dry milk	2½ tbs.	¼ cup	5 tbs.
yeast	1 tsp.	1½ tsp.	2½ tsp.

Grind some shredded wheat cereal in a food processor until finely crumbled. Or put it in a ziplock bag and crush with a rolling pin.

Variation: CRACKED SHREDDED WHEAT BREAD

Substitute ⅓ cup, ½ cup, ⅔ cup (respectively) of bread flour with cracked wheat. Add cracked wheat to liquid ingredients 1 hour prior to making bread.

GRAPE NUT BREAD

A nutty, flavorful, crunchy bread. This is similar, in some ways, to Cracked Wheat Bread.

	Small	Medium	Large
water	2/3 cup	1 cup	1 1/3 cups
vegetable oil	1 1/3 tbs.	2 tbs.	2 2/3 tbs.
sugar	2 tsp.	1 tbs.	1 1/3 tbs.
salt	1 tsp.	1 1/2 tsp.	2 tsp.
Grape Nuts cereal	1/3 cup	1/2 cup	2/3 cup
bread flour	1 1/3 cups	2 cups	2 2/3 cups
yeast	1 tsp.	1 1/2 tsp.	2 1/2 tsp.

GRITS BREAD

This is a must try for lovers of grits, Southern or not!

	Small	Medium	Large
water	1½ tbs.	2 tbs.	3 tbs.
margarine	¾ tbs.	1 tbs.	1½ tbs.
salt	⅓ tsp.	½ tsp.	¾ tsp.
sugar	1½ tsp.	2 tsp.	1 tbs.
cooked grits	¾ cup	1 cup	1½ cups
bread flour	1⅛ cups	1½ cups	2¼ cups
yeast	1 tsp.	1½ tsp.	2½ tsp.

KASHI

While usually found in the cereal section of a grocery store, Kashi is actually a combination of seven grain berries. Several different cereals are sold by the same company; make sure you purchase the "breakfast pilaf" which requires cooking. Kashi may also be found in health food stores. The kashi requires approximately 30 minutes to cook in a water/grain ratio of 2:1.

	Small	Medium	Large
water	½ cup	¾ cup	1 cup
margarine	⅔ tbs.	1 tbs.	1⅓ tbs.
brown sugar	1 tbs.	1½ tbs.	2 tbs.
salt	⅔ tsp.	1 tsp.	1⅓ tsp.
cooked kashi	⅓ cup	½ cup	⅔ cup
whole wheat flour	⅓ cup	½ cup	⅔ cup
bread flour	1⅓ cups	2 cups	2⅔ cups
yeast	1 tsp.	1½ tsp.	2½ tsp.

NEW YORK RYE

Tastes just like purchased New York rye. This is my rye bread tasters' favorite.

	Small	Medium	Large
water	½ cup+1 tbs.	1 cup-2 tbs.	1 cup+2 tbs.
vegetable oil	2 tsp.	1 tbs.	1⅓ tbs.
honey	1 tbs.	1½ tbs.	2 tbs.
salt	½ tsp.	¾ tsp.	1 tsp.
caraway seeds	1⅓ tsp.	2 tsp.	2⅔ tsp.
rye flour	⅔ cup	1 cup	1⅓ cups
bread flour	1 cup+1½ tbs.	1¾ cups	2⅓ cups
vital gluten, optional	2 tbs.	3 tbs.	¼ cup
nonfat dry milk	2 tbs.	3 tbs.	¼ cup
yeast	1 tsp.	1½ tsp.	2½ tsp.

Note: If dough appears crumbly or dry, add 1 tablespoon of water at a time while dough is kneading until a round ball is formed.

SWEDISH RYE BREAD

The taste is a cross between rye and whole wheat with a slight flavor of orange. Very good.

	Small	Medium	Large
water	½ cup+1 tbs.	1 cup-2 tbs.	1 cup+2 tbs.
honey	2½ tbs.	¼ cup	5 tbs.
margarine/butter	⅔ tbs.	1 tbs.	1⅓ tbs.
salt	1 tsp.	1½ tsp.	2 tsp.
caraway seeds	1⅓ tsp.	2 tsp.	2⅔ tsp.
grated orange peel	⅓ tsp.	½ tsp.	⅔ tsp.
rye flour	⅔ cup	1 cup	1⅓ cups
bread flour	1 cup	1½ cups	2 cups
yeast	1 tsp.	1½ tsp.	2½ tsp.

NORWEGIAN RYE BREAD

This is my favorite rye.

	Small	Medium	Large
water	½ cup	¾ cup	1 cup
molasses	3 tbs.	⅓ cup	6 tbs.
margarine/butter	1¼ tbs.	2 tbs.	2½ tbs.
salt	⅛ tsp.	¼ tsp.	⅓ tsp.
caraway seeds	1⅓ tsp.	2 tsp.	2⅔ tsp.
whole wheat flour	2½ tbs.	¼ cup	5 tbs.
rye flour	¾ cup+2 tbs.	1⅓ cups	1¾ cups
bread flour	1 cup-1½ tbs.	1¼ cups	1⅔ cups
yeast	1 tsp.	1½ tsp.	2½ tsp.

LIGHT PUMPERNICKEL

A wonderful, light pumpernickel — makes great sandwiches.

	Small	Medium	Large
water	2/3 cup	1 cup	1 1/3 cups
vegetable oil	1 1/3 tbs.	2 tbs.	2 2/3 tbs.
molasses	1 1/3 tbs.	2 tbs.	2 2/3 tbs.
gluten, optional	2 tsp.	1 tbs.	1 1/3 tbs.
sugar	2 tsp.	1 tbs.	1 1/3 tbs.
salt	1/2 tsp.	3/4 tsp.	1 tsp.
caraway seeds	1 1/4 tsp.	2 tsp.	2 1/2 tsp.
unsweetened cocoa	1 1/3 tbs.	2 tbs.	2 2/3 tbs.
rye flour	1 cup	1 1/2 cups	2 cups
bread flour	1 cup	1 1/2 cups	2 cups
yeast	1 tsp.	1 1/2 tsp.	2 1/2 tsp.

DARK PUMPERNICKEL

This is a heavy, dense bread which is terrific with soup and/or salad.

	Small	Medium	Large
water	⅔ cup	1 cup	1⅓ cups
vegetable oil	1⅓ tbs.	2 tbs.	2⅔ tbs.
molasses	2 tbs.	3 tbs.	¼ cup
unsweetened cocoa	1 tbs.	1½ tbs.	2 tbs.
brown sugar	2 tsp.	1 tbs.	1⅓ tbs.
instant coffee granules	⅔ tsp.	1 tsp.	1⅓ tsp.
salt	⅔ tsp.	1 tsp.	1⅓ tsp.
caraway seeds	1¼ tsp.	2 tsp.	2½ tsp.
rye flour	½ cup	¾ cup	1 cup
whole wheat flour	½ cup	¾ cup	1 cup
bread flour	1 cup	1½ cups	2 cups
yeast	1 tsp.	1½ tsp.	2½ tsp.

RUSSIAN BLACK BREAD

Eat this wonderful hearty bread with soup and/or salad or serve it as an appetizer with a crab dip! You may substitute dark molasses for the barley malt syrup.

	Small	Medium	Large
water	2/3 cup	1 cup	1 1/3 cups
vegetable oil	1 1/3 tbs.	2 tbs.	2 2/3 tbs.
barley malt syrup	2 tsp.	1 tbs.	1 1/3 tbs.
vinegar	2 tsp.	1 tbs.	1 1/3 tbs.
sugar	1/3 tsp.	1/2 tsp.	2/3 tsp.
salt	1/2 tsp.	3/4 tsp.	1 tsp.
unsweetened cocoa	1 tbs.	1 1/2 tbs.	2 tbs.
minced dried onion	1/4 tsp.	1/3 tsp.	1/2 tsp.
instant coffee granules	1/2 tsp.	3/4 tsp.	1 tsp.
caraway seed	1 1/3 tsp.	2 tsp.	2 2/3 tsp.
fennel	dash	1/8 tsp.	1/4 tsp.
oat bran	1/3 cup	1/2 cup	2/3 cup
bread flour	1 cup	1 1/2 cups	2 cups
rye flour	2/3 cup	1 cup	1 1/3 cups
yeast	1 tsp.	1 1/2 tsp.	2 1/2 tsp.

CORNMEAL BREAD

Wonderful with a Southern or Mexican meal — if it makes it to the table.

	Small	**Medium**	**Large**
water	2/3 cup	1 cup	1 1/3 cups
vegetable oil	2 1/2 tbs.	1/4 cup	5 tbs.
eggs	1/2	1	1 1/2
sugar	1 1/3 tbs.	2 tbs.	2 2/3 tbs.
salt	2/3 tsp.	1 tsp.	1 1/3 tsp.
yellow cornmeal	2/3 cup	1 cup	1 1/3 cups
bread flour	1 1/3 cups	2 cups	2 2/3 cups
yeast	1 tsp.	1 1/2 tsp.	2 1/2 tsp.

Variation: If you can find it in your health food store, try blue cornmeal. What a tasty, different treat. My bread testers thought at first that I was kidding but asked for more after trying it.

HONEY CORNMEAL BREAD

A very tasty, slightly sweet cornmeal loaf.

	Small	Medium	Large
water	½ cup	¾ cup	1 cup
vegetable oil	1 tbs.	1½ tbs.	2 tbs.
honey	2 tbs.	3 tbs.	¼ cup
eggs	2	3	4
salt	1 tsp.	1½ tsp.	2 tsp.
cornmeal	⅔ cup	1 cup	1⅓ cup
whole wheat flour	⅓ cup	½ cup	⅔ cup
bread flour	1 cup	1½ cups	2 cups
yeast	1 tsp.	1½ tsp.	2½ tsp.

CORNMEAL WHEAT GERM

A very good bread — great toasted.

	Small	Medium	Large
water	2/3 cup	1 cup	1 1/3 cup
vegetable oil	2 tsp.	1 tbs.	1 1/3 tbs.
honey	1 tbs.	1 1/2 tbs.	2 tbs.
cornmeal	1/3 cup	1/2 cup	2/3 cup
wheat germ	2 1/2 tbs.	1/4 cup	1/3 cup
bread flour	1 1/2 cups	2 1/4 cups	3 cups
yeast	1 tsp.	1 1/2 tsp.	2 1/2 tsp.

RICE BRAN BREAD

This is absolutely delicious. The rice bran and flour give this a slightly sweet taste. It is said that rice bran has the same cholesterol-lowering qualities as oat bran, so rice bran may be found in your grocery store. Otherwise, it may be purchased in health food stores.

	Small	Medium	Large
water	2/3 cup	1 cup	1 1/3 cups
margarine/butter	1 1/4 tbs.	2 tbs.	2 1/2 tbs.
sugar	2 tsp.	1 tbs.	1 1/3 tbs.
salt	1 tsp.	1 1/2 tsp.	2 tsp.
gluten, optional	2 tsp.	1 tbs.	1 1/3 tbs.
rice bran	1/3 cup	1/2 cup	2/3 cup
rice flour	1/3 cup	1/2 cup	2/3 cup
bread flour	1 1/3 cups	2 cups	2 2/3 cups
yeast	1 tsp.	1 1/2 tsp.	2 1/2 tsp.

BARLEY BREAD

A delicious, light airy bread. Molasses may be used as a substitute for the barley malt syrup.

	Small	Medium	Large
water	2/3 cup	1 cup	1 1/3 cups
margarine/butter	1 1/4 tbs.	2 tbs.	2 1/2 tbs.
barley malt syrup	2 tbs.	3 tbs.	1/4 cup
sugar	3 tbs.	1/3 cup	6 tbs.
salt	1 tsp.	1 1/2 tsp.	2 tsp.
cinnamon	2/3 tsp.	1 tsp.	1 1/3 tsp.
barley flour	1/3 cup	1/2 cup	2/3 cup
bread flour	1 2/3 cups	2 1/2 cups	3 1/3 cups
nonfat dry milk	1 tbs.	1 1/2 tbs.	2 tbs.
yeast	1 tsp.	1 1/2 tsp.	2 1/2 tsp.

BUCKWHEAT BREAD

This is a strong tasting bread — a must for buckwheat lovers.

	Small	Medium	Large
water	⅔ cup	1 cup	1⅓ cups
vegetable oil	1 tbs.	1½ tbs.	2 tbs.
honey	2 tsp.	1 tbs.	1⅓ tbs.
salt	½ tsp.	¾ tsp.	1 tsp.
buckwheat flour	⅓ cup	½ cup	⅔ cup
whole wheat flour	⅔ cup	1 cup	1⅓ cups
bread flour	1 cup	1½ cups	2 cups
nonfat dry milk	2 tbs.	3 tbs.	¼ cup
yeast	1 tsp.	1½ tsp.	2½ tsp.

BUCKWHEAT CORNMEAL BREAD

This wonderful mixture of buckwheat with cornmeal is one I think you'll like.

	Small	Medium	Large
water	⅔ cup	1 cup	1⅓ cup
margarine/butter	2 tbs.	3 tbs.	¼ cup
eggs	½	1	1½
salt	1 tsp.	1½ tsp.	2 tsp.
brown sugar	1 tbs.	1½ tbs.	2 tbs.
cornmeal	⅔ cup	1 cup	1⅓ cup
buckwheat flour	⅓ cup	½ cup	⅔ cup
bread flour	1 cup	1½ cups	2 cups
nonfat dry milk	2 tbs.	3 tbs.	¼ cup
yeast	1 tsp.	1½ tsp.	2½ tsp.

SOY FLAKES BREAD

The soy flakes give this bread a very unique texture and crunch. Kids love it. Soy flakes may be purchased at a local health food store. I keep them on hand to add to homemade granola.

	Small	Medium	Large
water	2/3 cup	1 cup	1 1/3 cups
vegetable oil	1 1/3 tbs.	2 tbs.	2 2/3 tbs.
sugar	1 1/3 tbs.	2 tbs.	2 2/3 tbs.
salt	2/3 tsp.	1 tsp.	1 1/3 tsp.
soy flakes	1/3 cup	1/2 cup	2/3 cup
bread flour	1 2/3 cups	2 1/2 cups	2 1/3 cups
yeast	1 tsp.	1 1/2 tsp.	2 1/2 tsp.

AMARANTH BREAD

Amaranth has a very unusual, distinct taste which is quite good and it is, of course, extremely nutritious. This is wonderful toasted.

	Small	Medium	Large
water	1 cup-1½ tbs.	1¼ cups	1⅔ cups
margarine/butter	2 tbs.	3 tbs.	¼ cup
sugar	2 tsp.	1 tbs.	1⅓ tbs.
salt	⅔ tsp.	1 tsp.	1⅓ tsp.
amaranth flour	⅓ cup	½ cup	⅔ cup
bread flour	1⅔ cups	2½ cups	3⅓ cups
nonfat dry milk	2 tbs.	3 tbs.	¼ cup
yeast	1 tsp.	1½ tsp.	2½ tsp.

AMARANTH CEREAL BREAD

If you have never tried amaranth, this is a good bread for you. I use the amaranth cereal made by Health Valley which can be found in a health food store or in some grocery stores. Other amaranth cereals will work also. This is a must try if looking for something a little different.

	Small	Medium	Large
water	2/3 cup	1 cup	1 1/3 cups
vegetable oil	2 tbs.	3 tbs.	1/4 cup
sugar	1 tbs.	1 1/2 tbs.	2 tbs.
salt	1 tsp.	1 1/2 tsp.	2 tsp.
amaranth cereal	1/2 cup	3/4 cup	1 cup
bread flour	1 1/2 cups	2 1/4 cups	3 cups
yeast	1 tsp.	1 1/2 tsp.	2 1/2 tsp.

AMARANTH NUT BREAD

A wonderful nutty bread. Although it may be used for sandwiches, this is more of a dessert bread, I think.

	Small	Medium	Large
water	2/3 cup	1 cup	1 1/3 cups
vegetable oil	1 1/3 tbs.	2 tbs.	2 2/3 tbs.
honey	2 tbs.	3 tbs.	1/4 cup
eggs	1/2	1	1 1/2
vanilla extract	2/3 tsp.	1 tsp.	1 1/3 tsp.
salt	2/3 tsp.	1 tsp.	1 1/4 tsp.
amaranth flour	1/3 cup	1/2 cup	2/3 cup
bread flour	1 2/3 cup	2 1/2 cups	3 1/3 cups
nonfat dry milk	2 tbs.	3 tbs.	1/4 cup
yeast	1 tsp.	1 1/2 tsp.	2 1/2 tsp.

At beep add: (If National/Panasonic add following first kneading)

| chopped walnuts | 1/3 cup | 1/2 cup | 2/3 cup |

THREE SEED BREAD

A wonderful taste and texture. Feel free to experiment with different seeds. Try combinations of anise, fennel, caraway or any other seeds which you may have on hand!

	Small	**Medium**	**Large**
water	3/4 cup	1 1/8 cups	1 1/2 cups
vegetable oil	1 tbs.	1 1/2 tbs.	2 tbs.
honey	1 tsp.	1 1/2 tsp.	2 tsp.
salt	1/3 tsp.	1/2 tsp.	2/3 tsp.
sunflower seeds	2 tbs.	3 tbs.	4 tbs.
sesame seeds	1 tbs.	1 1/2 tbs.	2 tbs.
poppy seeds	2 tsp.	1 tbs.	1 1/3 tbs.
whole wheat flour	2/3 cup	1 cup	1 1/3 cups
bread flour	1 1/3 cups	2 cups	2 2/3 cups
nonfat dry milk	2 tbs.	3 tbs.	1/4 cup
yeast	1 tsp.	1 1/2 tsp.	2 1/2 tsp.

ANCIENT GRAIN BREAD

*This bread is a variation of **Three Seed Bread**, page 84. Great texture. A unique bread with the wonderful tastes of quinoa, amaranth, sesame seeds and poppy seeds. The quinoa and amaranth make this an extremely nutritious, healthy bread. In place of the seeds in **Three Seed Bread**, substitute:*

	Small	Medium	Large
quinoa grains	1⅓ tbs.	2 tbs.	2⅔ tbs.
amaranth grains	1⅓ tbs.	2 tbs.	2⅔ tbs.
sesame seeds	2 tsp.	1 tbs.	1⅓ tbs.
poppy seeds	1¼ tsp.	2 tsp.	2½ tsp.

QUINOA BREAD

The quinoa gives this bread a nutty flavor. Great source of protein and calcium — worth trying. Ancient Harvest packages quinoa flour and it should be available through a good health food store.

	Small	Medium	Large
water	¾ cup	1⅛ cups	1½ cups
margarine/butter	2½ tbs.	¼ cup	5 tbs.
sugar	1⅓ tsp.	2 tsp.	2⅔ tsp.
salt	⅔ tsp.	1 tsp.	1⅓ tsp.
quinoa flour	⅓ cup	½ cup	⅔ cup
bread flour	1⅔ cups	2½ cups	3½ cups
yeast	1 tsp.	1½ tsp.	2½ tsp.

SOURDOUGH BREADS

As the early day pioneers traveled west across the United States, they carried a mixture of flour and milk or water which was used to leaven bread. As the mixture or starter aged, it became more sour and, hence, so did the bread.

A true sourdough starter is nothing more than the flour and milk or water which sits at room temperature for several days and catches live yeast bacteria from the air. Most starter recipes today include yeast as an original ingredient as it is much easier and less time consuming. In addition, many sourdough bread recipes also indicate usage of yeast itself as it does provide a higher rising, lighter loaf.

A sourdough starter should be kept in a glass or plastic bowl which has a tight fitting lid. I recommend a bowl instead of a jar as you can "feed" your starter right in the bowl easily. To make your starter, mix together:

2 cups lukewarm milk
2 cups bread flour
2½ tsp. (one package) yeast

I mix the starter with an electric, hand-held mixer on the lowest setting. Cover your starter and place in a warm, draft-free location for 4 to 7 days, gently stirring it once a day. You may notice that the mixture bubbles and in some cases it may even overflow your bowl. This is an indication that you have a healthy fermenting process going on. A sour smelling liquid may form on top of the starter which should simply be poured off and discarded.

If your starter ever changes colors, to purple, for example, discard and start another one.

After allowing your starter to sit for 4 to 7 days it is ready to be used. Take out whatever portion your recipe calls for and put into the machine as you would any liquid ingredient. After removing a portion from the starter, the starter must be "fed." Simply add equal portions of milk or water and flour as was used. For example, if you used 1 cup of starter, replace it with 1 cup of water and 1 cup of bread flour.

Some hints on feeding your starter: always use the same kind of flour. If you used bread flour in your original starter, use bread flour to feed it. Also, alternate between milk and water for each feeding. Since your original liquid ingredient was milk, the first liquid feeding should be with water. If you forget which you used last, that's okay, but try to alternate at least every other time. After feeding your starter, let it sit at room temperature for approximately 1 day and then refrigerate.

Many cookbooks suggest stirring the starter once a day even when being refrigerated; I find that it is not necessary. You must, however, use a portion of the starter at least once a week. If you choose not to bake sourdough breads that often, then remove a cup of your starter and feed it as though you used some during the week. If this is not done, your starter will turn rancid and have to be replaced. Should you be away on vacation or otherwise unable to tend to the starter, freeze it. Upon your return, thaw it in the refrigerator and then remove a portion and feed it as soon as you are able.

You may be thinking that this sounds too complicated, but it really is not, nor is the starter overly fragile. A friend of mine had the same starter for 14 years!

My first few loaves of sourdough were not very sour and I feared it was my starter. After allowing the starter to mellow a little by sitting in the refrigerator and using only once a week, it and the breads became more sour.

Another hint is to put the bread in on the timer cycle for early morning baking. The milk put in the night before adds a little more sour taste. If the bread is getting too sour for you, feed with water more often than milk.

SOURDOUGH BREAD

This compares favorably to the famous San Francisco sourdoughs.

	Small	Medium	Large
starter	3⁄4 cup	1 cup	1 1⁄2 cups
milk	6 tbs.	2⁄3 cup	3⁄4 cup
margarine/butter	1 1⁄4 tbs.	2 tbs.	2 1⁄2 tbs.
sugar	1 1⁄3 tbs.	2 tbs.	2 2⁄3 tbs.
salt	2 tsp.	1 tbs.	1 1⁄3 tbs.
bread flour	2 cups	3 cups	4 cups
yeast	1 tsp.	1 1⁄2 tsp.	2 1⁄2 tsp.

SOURDOUGH WHEAT BREAD

A delicious sourdough with the benefits of whole wheat flour.

	Small	Medium	Large
starter	¾ cup	1 cup	1½ cups
milk	6 tbs.	⅔ cup	¾ cup
margarine/butter	1¼ tbs.	2 tbs.	2½ tbs.
sugar	1⅓ tbs.	2 tbs.	2⅔ tbs.
salt	2 tsp.	1 tbs.	1⅓ tbs.
whole wheat flour	¾ cup	1 cup	1½ cups
bread flour	1¼ cups	2 cups	2½ cups
yeast	1 tsp.	1½ tsp.	2½ tsp.

SOURDOUGH FRENCH BREAD

This is absolutely delicious — great for sandwiches.

	Small	Medium	Large
starter	⅔ cup	1 cup	1⅓ cups
water	6 tbs.	⅔ cup	¾ cup
sugar	1 tsp.	1½ tsp.	2 tsp.
salt	⅔ tsp.	1 tsp.	1⅓ tsp.
bread flour	2 cups	3 cups	4 cups
yeast	1 tsp.	1½ tsp.	2½ tsp.

SOURDOUGH PIZZA CRUST

This is an interesting change-of-pace in pizza making. Make this on the dough setting.

	Small	Medium	Large
water	1 cup-1 tbs.	1¼ cups	1⅔ cups
starter	½ cup	¾ cup	1 cup
olive oil	1½ tbs.	2¼ tbs.	3 tbs.
salt	½ tsp.	¾ tsp.	1 tsp.
all purpose flour	2 cups	3 cups	4 cups
yeast	1 tsp.	1½ tsp.	2½ tsp.

Roll dough into rectangle or circle, depending on pan to be used. Place on pan and turn excess under, forming a raised edge. Brush very lightly with olive oil. Cover and let rise about 30 minutes. Top with pizza sauce and desired toppings. Place in a cold oven, turn temperature up to 450° and bake until crust is brown and cheese is melted, 30 to 45 minutes.

SOURDOUGH CORNMEAL BREAD

A very unique, delicious bread.

	Small	Medium	Large
starter	2/3 cup	1 cup	1 1/3 cups
milk	2/3 cup	1 cup	1 1/3 cups
egg, optional	1/2	1	1 1/2
margarine/butter	1 tbs.	1 1/2 tbs.	2 tbs.
baking soda	1/8 tsp.	1/4 tsp.	1/2 tsp.
sugar	1 tbs.	1 1/2 tbs.	2 tbs.
salt	1/2 tsp.	3/4 tsp.	1 tsp.
cornmeal	2/3 cup	1 cup	1 1/3 cups
bread flour	1 1/3 cups	2 cups	2 2/3 cups
yeast	1 tsp.	1 1/2 tsp.	2 1/2 tsp.

SOURDOUGH OATMEAL BREAD

This is a very moist sourdough bread.

	Small	Medium	Large
starter	½ cup	¾ cup	1 cup
milk	¾ cup	1 cup	1½ cups
margarine/butter	1 tbs.	1½ tbs.	2 tbs.
sugar	2 tsp.	1 tbs.	1⅓ tbs.
salt	1 tsp.	1½ tsp.	2 tsp.
oats	½ cup	¾ cup	1 cup
bread flour	1½ cups	2¼ cups	3 cups
yeast	1 tsp.	1½ tsp.	2½ tsp.

SOURDOUGH RYE BREAD

A very light, slightly sour loaf of rye. This is somewhat different than many of the other sourdoughs as it has its own starter, which is used in its entirety in the recipe. Molasses may be substituted for the barley malt syrup.

Starter*:	Small	Medium	Large
warm milk (115°)	½ cup	¾ cup	1 cup
rye flour	½ cup	¾ cup	1 cup
yeast	⅔ tsp.	1 tsp.	1⅓ tsp.

To prepare the starter: sprinkle yeast over warm milk and stir until dissolved; then stir in the rye flour. Cover and let stand at room temperature for 3 days, stirring once a day. Use the entire starter in your bread recipe on the next page.

Bread:	Small	Medium	Large
rye starter	*	*	*
water	1/3 cup	1/2 cup	2/3 cup
egg	1/2	1	1 1/2
vegetable oil	1 tbs.	1 1/2 tbs.	2 tbs.
barley malt syrup	1 tbs.	1 1/2 tbs.	2 tbs.
salt	1 tsp.	1 1/2 tsp.	2 tsp.
caraway seeds	2 tsp.	1 tbs.	1 1/3 tbs.
bread flour	1 1/2 cups	2 1/4 cups	3 cups
rye flour	1/2 cup	3/4 cup	1 cup
yeast	1 tsp.	1 1/2 tsp.	2 1/2 tsp.

FRUIT AND VEGETABLE BREADS

APPLE BUTTER BREAD

Bake the apple butter right into the bread. Try substituting any favorite jam or jelly for the apple butter.

	Small	Medium	Large
water	2/3 cup	1 cup	1 1/3 cups
vegetable oil	1 1/3 tbs.	2 tbs.	2 2/3 tbs.
apple butter	1/3 cup	1/2 cup	2/3 cup
sugar	2 tsp.	1 tbs.	1 1/3 tbs.
salt	2/3 tsp.	1 tsp.	1 1/3 tsp.
whole wheat flour	2/3 cup	1 cup	1 1/3 cups
bread flour	1 1/3 cups	2 cups	2 2/3 cups
yeast	1 tsp.	1 1/2 tsp.	2 1/2 tsp.

APPLE CHUNK BREAD

You'll think you're eating an apple pie. This is an "absolute must try." The apple chunks give it a wonderful sweetness. This dessert bread should be served warm (it probably won't last long enough to get cold anyway).

	Small	Medium	Large
milk	½ cup	⅔ cup	1 cup
vegetable oil	2 tbs.	2½ tbs.	¼ cup
sugar	1 tbs.	1¼ tbs.	2 tbs.
cinnamon	¼ tsp.	⅓ tsp.	½ tsp.
salt	¾ tsp.	1 tsp.	1½ tsp.
bread flour	1½ cups	2 cups	3 cups
yeast	1 tsp.	1½ tsp.	2½ tsp.

At beep add: (If National/Panasonic add following first kneading)

medium apple, peeled and diced:	⅔	1	1⅓

APPLESAUCE BREAD

This bread made a huge hit at a neighborhood potluck — especially the children kept going back for more. Very moist.

	Small	Medium	Large
applesauce	2/3 cup	1 cup	1 1/3 cup
margarine/butter	1 1/4 tbs.	2 tbs.	2 1/2 tbs.
sugar	2 tsp.	1 tbs.	1 1/3 tbs.
salt	2/3 tsp.	1 tsp.	1 1/3 tsp.
cinnamon, optional	2/3 tsp.	1 tsp.	1 1/3 tsp.
whole wheat flour	1/2 cup	3/4 cup	1 cup
bread flour	1 cup	1 1/2 cups	2 cups
yeast	1 tsp.	1 1/2 tsp.	2 1/2 tsp.

BANANA OATMEAL BREAD

A slight taste of banana with the "feel" of oatmeal. The flavor of the banana seems to be stronger when the bread is toasted.

	Small	Medium	Large
water	1/3 cup	1/2 cup	2/3 cup
mashed banana	1/2 cup	3/4 cup	1 cup
vegetable oil	1 1/4 tbs.	2 tbs.	2 1/2 tbs.
sugar	2 tsp.	1 tbs.	1 1/3 tbs.
salt	2/3 tsp.	1 tsp.	1 1/3 tsp.
oats	2/3 cup	1 cup	1 1/3 cups
bread flour	1 1/3 cups	2 cups	2 2/3 cups
yeast	1 tsp.	1 1/2 tsp.	2 1/2 tsp.

BLUEBERRY BREAD

Delicious — try blue cornmeal although yellow will do nicely too. If using frozen blueberries, they must be well thawed and tightly packed into your measuring cup.

	Small	Medium	Large
water	2½ tbs.	¼ cup	5 tbs.
cottage cheese	⅓ cup	½ cup	⅔ cup
margarine/butter	1 tbs.	1½ tbs.	2 tbs.
blueberries	½ cup	¾ cup	1 cup
sugar	1⅓ tbs.	2 tbs.	2⅔ tbs.
salt	1 tsp.	1½ tsp.	2 tsp.
blue cornmeal	⅔ cup	1 cup	1⅓ cups
bread flour	1⅓ cups	2 cups	2⅔ cups
yeast	1 tsp.	1½ tsp.	2½ tsp.

CARROT BREAD

A delicious, healthy bread. A good way to get your beta carotene!

	Small	Medium	Large
water	½ cup	¾ cup	1 cup
vegetable oil	2 tsp.	1 tbs.	1⅓ tbs.
grated carrot	⅓ cup	½ cup	⅔ cup
brown sugar	1 tbs.	1½ tbs.	2 tbs.
salt	⅔ tsp.	1 tsp.	1⅓ tsp.
oats	⅔ cup	1 cup	1⅓ cups
whole wheat flour	⅓ cup	½ cups	⅔ cups
bread flour	1 cup	1½ cups	2 cups
nonfat dry milk	2 tbs.	3 tbs.	¼ cup
yeast	2½ tsp.	2½ tsp.	2½ tsp.

COCONUT PINEAPPLE BREAD

Wonderful. A must for Sunday brunch or dessert. Fun for a "Hawaiian Luau" dinner.

	Small	Medium	Large
milk	2 tbs.	2½ tbs.	¼ cup
cream cheese	½ cup	⅔ cup	1 cup
can (8 oz.) crushed, drained pineapple	½ can	⅔ can	1 can
pineapple extract	1 tsp.	1⅓ tsp.	2 tsp.
vegetable oil	2 tbs.	2½ tbs.	¼ cup
sugar	1½ tbs.	2 tbs.	3 tbs.
salt	½ tsp.	⅔ tsp.	1 tsp.
grated coconut	2 tbs.	2½ tbs.	¼ cup
bread flour	1½ cups	2 cups	3 cups
yeast	1 tsp.	1½ tsp.	2½ tsp.

LEMON BREAD

This bread has a subtle, pleasing flavor.

	Small	Medium	Large
water	⅔ cup	1 cup	1⅓ cups
margarine/butter	1¼ tbs.	2 tbs.	2½ tbs.
grated lemon peel	⅔ tsp.	1 tsp.	1⅓ tsp.
sugar	⅓ tsp.	½ tsp.	⅔ tsp.
salt	⅓ tsp.	½ tsp.	⅔ tsp.
bread flour	2 cups	3 cups	4 cups
nonfat dry milk	2 tbs.	¼ cup	5 tbs.
yeast	2½ tsp.	2½ tsp.	2½ tsp.

ONION BREAD

Even if you typically do not like onions, you'll like this bread. It is a great accompaniment to barbecue dinners — chicken or burgers.

	Small	Medium	Large
water	½ cup	¾ cup	1 cup
margarine/butter	1 tbs.	1½ tbs.	2 tbs.
grated fresh onion	⅓ cup	½ cup	⅔ cup
sugar	2 tsp.	1 tbs.	1⅓ tbs.
salt	⅔ tsp.	1 tsp.	1⅓ tsp.
whole wheat flour	⅓ cup	½ cup	⅔ cup
bread flour	1⅔ cups	2½ cups	3⅓ cups
nonfat dry milk	1 tbs.	1½ tbs.	2 tbs.
yeast	1 tsp.	1½ tsp.	2½ tsp.

ORANGE BANANA BREAD

This unique breakfast bread is just as good toasted as fresh out of the oven.

	Small	Medium	Large
orange juice	6 tbs.	½ cup	¾ cup
margarine/butter	1½ tsp.	2 tsp.	1 tbs.
mashed banana	¼ cup	⅓ cup	½ cup
sugar	1½ tsp.	2 tsp.	1 tbs.
grated orange peel	¼ tsp.	⅓ tsp.	½ tsp.
salt	½ tsp.	⅔ tsp.	1 tsp.
bread flour	1½ cups	2 cups	3 cups
yeast	1 tsp.	1½ tsp.	2½ tsp.

ORANGE CINNAMON BREAD

Delicious breakfast bread. Set it on the timer cycle and wake up to it hot from the oven, or have it toasted the next day, if it lasts that long.

	Small	Medium	Large
orange juice	½ cup	⅔ cup	1 cup
margarine/butter	1 tbs.	1¼ tbs.	2 tbs.
cinnamon	1 tsp.	1¼ tsp.	2 tsp.
grated orange peel	½ tsp.	⅔ tsp.	1 tsp.
salt	⅓ tsp.	½ tsp.	¾ tsp.
sugar	1 tsp.	1¼ tsp.	2 tsp.
bread flour	1½ cups	2 cups	3 cups
yeast	1 tsp.	1½ tsp.	2½ tsp.

PEANUT BUTTER AND JELLY BREAD

The taste of peanut butter and jelly WITH NO MESS!!! A parent's favorite. This is a wonderful, moist bread with all the nutrition of whole wheat.

	Small	Medium	Large
water	⅔ cup	1 cup	1⅓ cups
vegetable oil	1 tbs.	1½ tbs.	2 tbs.
peanut butter	⅓ cup	½ cup	⅔ cup
jelly	⅓ cup	½ cup	⅔ cup
sugar	2 tsp.	1 tbs.	1⅓ tbs.
salt	⅔ tsp.	1 tsp.	1⅓ tsp.
whole wheat flour	⅔ cup	1 cup	1⅓ cups
bread flour	1⅓ cups	2 cups	2⅔ cups
yeast	1 tsp.	1½ tsp.	2½ tsp.

POPPY SEED BREAD

A very light, airy bread; eat it alone or try it topped with hot ham and cheese.

	Small	Medium	Large
water	½ cup	⅔ cup	1 cup
vegetable oil	2 tbs.	2½ tbs.	¼ cup
vanilla	½ tsp.	⅔ tsp.	1 tsp.
butter flavoring	½ tsp.	⅔ tsp.	1 tsp.
almond extract	½ tsp.	⅔ tsp.	1 tsp.
salt	½ tsp.	⅔ tsp.	1 tsp.
sugar	1½ tbs.	2 tbs.	3 tbs.
poppy seeds	1 tbs.	1¼ tbs.	2 tbs.
bread flour	1½ cups	2 cups	3 cups
yeast	1 tsp.	1½ tsp.	2½ tsp.

POTATO BREAD

Really good alone or as sandwich bread. The potatoes give it just a little extra flavor. Slices very well. Some people make potato bread by using instant potatoes. While I have not tried it, I understand that it, too, is quite tasty.

	Small	Medium	Large
potato water	6 tbs.	½ cup	¾ cup
margarine/butter	2 tbs.	2½ tbs.	¼ cup
egg	½	¾	1
mashed potatoes	¼ cup	⅓ cup	½ cup
sugar	1 tbs.	1¼ tbs.	2 tbs.
salt	½ tsp.	⅔ tsp.	1 tsp.
bread flour	1½ cups	2 cups	3 cups
yeast	1 tsp.	1½ tsp.	2½ tsp.

Start by boiling 1-2 peeled potatoes. Save the water to use in the bread. Then mash the potatoes, without milk or butter, and let cool to lukewarm or room temperature.

PUMPKIN/WINTER SQUASH BREAD

Spicy squash bread uses those leftover squashes. Great way to hide vegetables from finicky eaters. Canned pumpkin may be used if desired.

	Small	Medium	Large
water	½ cup	¾ cup	1 cup
winter squash*	6 tbs.	⅔ cup	¾ cup
vegetable oil	1⅓ tbs.	2 tbs.	2⅔ tbs.
honey	1⅓ tbs.	2 tbs.	2⅔ tbs.
salt	1 tsp.	1½ tsp.	2 tsp.
cinnamon	⅔ tsp.	1 tsp.	1⅓ tsp.
allspice	⅓ tsp.	½ tsp.	⅔ tsp.
nutmeg	⅛ tsp.	¼ tsp.	⅓ tsp.
ground cloves	⅛ tsp.	¼ tsp.	⅓ tsp.
whole wheat flour	⅓ cup	½ cup	⅔ cup
bread flour	1⅔ cups	2½ cups	3⅓ cups
yeast	1 tsp.	1½ tsp.	2½ tsp.

*Cooked, mashed squash such as pumpkin, butternut, acorn, etc.

RAISIN BREAD

A friend of mine tasted this bread and went out the next day to buy an automatic bread machine. Need I say more?

	Small	Medium	Large
water	½ cup+1 tbs.	¾ cup	1⅛ cups
margarine/butter	1 tbs.	1¼ tbs.	2 tbs.
sugar	1 tbs.	1⅓ tbs.	2 tbs.
salt	½ tsp.	⅔ tsp.	1 tsp.
bread flour	1½ cups	2 cups	3 cups
yeast	2½ tsp.	2½ tsp.	2½ tsp.

At beep add: (If National/Panasonic add following first kneading)

| raisins | 6 tbs. | ½ cup | ¾ cup |

Variations:

All ingredients are put in the machine when it beeps (or during the rest period after the first kneading in National or Panasonic machines).

	Small	Medium	Large
CINNAMON RAISIN			
raisins	6 tbs.	½ cup	¾ cup
cinnamon	1½ tsp.	2 tsp.	1 tbs.
APRICOT BREAD			
dried diced apricots	6 tbs.	½ cup	¾ cup
MIXED DRIED FRUIT			
dried mixed fruit, diced	6 tbs.	½ cup	¾ cup
ORANGE RAISIN			
raisins	6 tbs.	½ cup	¾ cup
grated orange peel	¼ tsp.	⅓ tsp.	½ tsp.

PISTACHIO RAISIN BREAD

You won't believe how good this one is!

	Small	Medium	Large
water	2/3 cup	1 cup	1 1/3 cups
vegetable oil	1 tbs.	1 1/2 tbs.	2 tbs.
honey	1 tbs.	1 1/2 tbs.	2 tbs.
salt	2/3 tsp.	1 tsp.	1 1/3 tsp.
whole wheat flour	1/2 cup	3/4 cup	1 cup
bread flour	1 1/2 cups	2 1/4 cups	3 cups
yeast	1 tsp.	1 1/2 tsp.	2 1/2 tsp.

At beep add: (If National/Panasonic add following first kneading)

	Small	Medium	Large
raisins	2 tbs.	3 tbs.	1/4 cup
pistachios	2 tbs.	3 tbs.	1/4 cup

IRISH SODA BREAD

While at first you may wonder about the caraway seed/raisin combination, once you've tried it, you'll be hooked. This is a "must try."

	Small	Medium	Large
water	½ cup	⅔ cup	1 cup
margarine/butter	1 tbs.	1¼ tbs.	2 tbs.
sugar	1 tbs.	1⅓ tbs.	2 tbs.
salt	½ tsp.	⅔ tsp.	1 tsp.
baking soda	¼ tsp.	⅓ tsp.	½ tsp.
caraway seeds	1 tbs.	1⅓ tsp.	2 tsp.
bread flour	1½ cups	2 cups	3 cups
buttermilk powder	1½ tbs.	2 tbs.	3 tbs.
yeast	1 tsp.	1½ tsp.	2½ tsp.

At beep add: (If National/Panasonic add following first kneading)

raisins	¼ cup	⅓ cup	½ cup

SUNFLOWER BREAD

The sunflower seeds are an interesting change from a raisin bread. Terrific flavor. Try substituting pumpkin seeds for another interesting, tasty variation.

	Small	Medium	Large
water	⅔ cup	1 cup	1⅓ cups
vegetable oil	1⅓ tbs.	2 tbs.	2⅔ tbs.
honey	1⅓ tbs.	2 tbs.	2⅔ tbs.
salt	½ tsp.	¾ tsp.	1 tsp.
oats	⅓ cup	½ cup	⅔ cup
whole wheat flour	⅓ cup	½ cup	⅔ cup
bread flour	1⅓ cups	2 cups	2⅔ cups
yeast	1 tsp.	1½ tsp.	2½ tsp.

At beep add: (If National/Panasonic add following first kneading)

	Small	Medium	Large
sunflower seeds	⅓ cup	½ cup	⅔ cup
raisins	2½ tbs.	¼ cup	5 tbs.

STOLLEN

	Small	Medium	Large
milk	6 tbs.	½ cup	¾ cup
margarine/butter	3 tbs.	¼ cup	⅓ cup
egg	¾	1	1½
almond extract	⅛ tsp.	¼ tsp.	⅓ tsp.
rum extract	⅛ tsp.	¼ tsp.	⅓ tsp.
sugar	¼ cup	⅓ cup	½ cup
salt	½ tsp.	¾ tsp.	1 tsp.
mace	⅛ tsp.	⅛ tsp.	¼ tsp.
cardamom	dash	dash	⅛ tsp.
grated lemon peel	1½ tsp.	2 tsp.	1 tbs.
grated orange peel	1½ tsp.	2 tsp.	1 tbs.
bread flour	1½ cups	2 cups	3 cups
yeast	2½ tsp.	2½ tsp.	2½ tsp.

At the beep add: (If National/Panasonic add following first kneading)

	Small	Medium	Large
golden raisins	¼ cup	⅓ cup	½ cup
currants	¼ cup	⅓ cup	½ cup
slivered almonds	¼ cup	⅓ cup	½ cup
mixed candied fruit	¼ cup	⅓ cup	½ cup

PANETTONE

	Small	Medium	Large
water	6 tbs.	½ cup	¾ cup
margarine/butter	2½ tbs.	¼ cup	⅓ cup
eggs	¾	1	1½
sugar	2½ tbs.	¼ cup	⅓ cup
salt	⅓ tsp.	½ tsp.	¾ tsp.
grated lemon peel	¾ tsp.	1 tsp.	1½ tsp.
bread flour	1½ cups	2 cups	3 cups
yeast	1 tsp.	1½ tsp.	2½ tsp.

At beep add: (If National/Panasonic add following first kneading)

	Small	Medium	Large
golden raisins	2½ tbs.	¼ cup	⅓ cup
candied fruit	2½ tbs.	¼ cup	⅓ cup
chopped nuts	2½ tbs.	¼ cup	⅓ cup

SALSA CORNMEAL BREAD

Wonderful cornmeal with just a hint of the hot and spicy salsa. Serve with any Mexican meal.

	Small	Medium	Large
milk	2/3 cup	1 cup	1 1/3 cups
salsa	2 1/2 tbs.	1/4 cup	5 tbs.
margarine/butter	1 1/4 tbs.	2 tbs.	2 1/2 tbs.
egg	1/2	1	1 1/2
sugar	2 tsp.	1 tbs.	1 1/3 tbs.
salt	2/3 tsp.	1 tsp.	1 1/3 tsp.
yellow cornmeal	2/3 cup	1 cup	1 1/3 cups
bread flour	1 1/3 cups	2 cups	2 2/3 cups
yeast	1 tsp.	1 1/2 tsp.	2 1/2 tsp.

STRAWBERRY BANANA BREAD

This wonderful, light loaf has just the right hint of both strawberries and banana.

	Small	Medium	Large
milk	¼ cup	⅓ cup	½ cup
mashed strawberries	¼ cup	⅓ cup	½ cup
mashed bananas	¼ cup	⅓ cup	½ cup
margarine	1 tbs.	1¼ tbs.	2 tbs.
sugar	1 tsp.	1¼ tsp.	2 tsp.
salt	1 tsp.	1¼ tsp.	2 tsp.
bread flour	1½ cups	2 cups	3 cups
yeast	1 tsp.	1½ tsp.	2½ tsp.

SWEET POTATO BREAD

Just a hint of sweet potatoes makes this a perfect accompaniment to a turkey dinner and later for the leftover sandwiches.

	Small	Medium	Large
sweet potato water	6 tbs.	½ cup	¾ cup
sweet potatoes	¼ cup	⅓ cup	½ cup
margarine/butter	2 tbs.	2½ tbs.	4 tbs.
brown sugar	1½ tbs.	2 tbs.	3 tbs.
salt	½ tsp.	⅔ tsp.	1 tsp.
bread flour	1½ cups	2 cups	3 cups
yeast	1 tsp.	1½ tsp.	2½ tsp.

ZUCCHINI WHEAT BREAD

Zucchini lovers will love this one. Toasting brings out a stronger flavor.

	Small	Medium	Large
shredded zucchini	½ cup	¾ cup	1 cup
water	½ cup	¾ cup	1 cup
vegetable oil	2 tbs.	3 tbs.	¼ cup
honey	2 tbs.	3 tbs.	¼ cup
salt	⅔ tsp.	1 tsp.	1⅓ tsp.
grated orange peel	⅔ tsp.	1 tsp.	1⅓ tsp.
wheat germ	2½ tsp.	¼ cup	5 tbs.
whole wheat flour	1 cup	1½ cups	2 cups
bread flour	1 cup	1½ cups	2 cups
yeast	1 tsp.	1½ tsp.	2½ tsp.

SPICE AND HERB BREADS

OREGANO BREAD

This is an absolute must with spaghetti or lasagna — an often requested bread. Once you have this you'll never go back to plain, old garlic bread! Several bread testers have "placed orders" for this when entertaining with Italian meals.

	Small	Medium	Large
water	5/8 cup	1 cup-1½ tbs.	1¼ cups
olive oil	2 tbs.	2½ tbs.	¼ cup
salt	1 tsp.	1⅓ tsp.	2 tsp.
Parmesan cheese, grated	2 tbs.	2½ tbs.	¼ cup
oregano	1½ tsp.	2 tsp.	1 tbs.
bread flour	1½ cups	2 cups	3 cups
nonfat dry milk	2½ tbs.	3 tbs.	⅓ cup
yeast	1 tsp.	1½ tsp.	2½ tsp.

HERB BREAD

A very spicy bread to perk up a meal. Good with chicken or fish.

	Small	Medium	Large
water	½ cup+1 tbs.	⅔ cup	1⅛ cups
egg	½	¾	1
margarine/butter	1 tbs.	1¼ tbs.	2 tbs.
salt	¼ tsp.	⅓ tsp.	½ tsp.
sugar	¼ tsp.	⅓ tsp.	½ tsp.
oregano	¼ tsp.	⅓ tsp.	½ tsp.
thyme	¼ tsp.	⅓ tsp.	½ tsp.
black pepper	¼ tsp.	⅓ tsp.	½ tsp.
dried parsley	¼ tsp.	⅓ tsp.	½ tsp.
celery seed	dash	dash	⅛ tsp.
sage	dash	dash	⅛ tsp.
wheat germ	2 tbs.	2½ tbs.	¼ cup
oats	2 tbs.	2½ tbs.	¼ cup
bread flour	1¼ cups	1⅔ cups	2½ cups
nonfat dry milk	1 tbs.	1¼ tbs.	2 tbs.
yeast	1 tsp.	1½ tsp.	2½ tsp.

PARSLEY HERB BREAD

This is another good bread to serve with chicken. Not as spicy as the preceding **Herb Bread***; but adds a nice flavor to the meal.*

	Small	Medium	Large
water	1 cup-1½ tbs.	1¼ cups	1⅔ cups
olive oil	2½ tbs.	¼ cup	5 tbs.
sugar	¼ tsp.	⅓ tsp.	½ tsp.
salt	1 tsp.	1⅓ tsp.	2 tsp.
parsley	1 tsp.	1⅓ tsp.	2 tsp.
chives	¼ tsp.	⅓ tsp.	½ tsp.
tarragon	¼ tsp.	⅓ tsp.	½ tsp.
bread flour	1½ cups	2 cups	3 cups
nonfat dry milk	2½ tbs.	3 tbs.	⅓ cup
yeast	1 tsp.	1½ tsp.	2½ tsp.

DILL BREAD

Outstanding bread — great with either pasta or fish. One of our favorites. Another often requested bread.

	Small	Medium	Large
cottage cheese	⅔ cup	1 cup	1⅓ cups
eggs	1½	2	2½
sugar	1⅓ tbs.	2 tbs.	2⅔ tbs.
dill weed	2 tsp.	1 tbs.	1⅓ tbs.
salt	⅔ tsp.	1 tsp.	1⅓ tsp.
baking soda	⅛ tsp.	¼ tsp.	⅓ tsp.
bread flour	1⅔ cups	2½ cups	3⅓ cups
yeast	1 tsp.	1½ tsp.	2½ tsp.

GARLIC PARMESAN BREAD

If you're a garlic bread lover, this is for you. Feel free to increase/decrease amount of garlic powder to suit your taste. Very aromatic and great, of course, with Italian meals.

	Small	Medium	Large
water	½ cup	¾ cup	1 cup
margarine/butter	1¼ tbs.	2 tbs.	2½ tbs.
honey	1⅓ tsp.	2 tsp.	2⅔ tsp.
salt	⅔ tsp.	1 tsp.	1⅓ tsp.
garlic powder	⅔ tsp.	1 tsp.	1⅓ tsp.
bread flour	1 cup+2½ tbs.	1½ cups	2⅓ cups
Parmesan cheese, grated	⅓ cup	½ cup	⅔ cup
nonfat dry milk	1¼ tbs.	2 tbs.	2½ tbs.
yeast	1 tsp.	1½ tsp.	2½ tsp.

ANADAMA BREAD

A very different tasting bread — the molasses gives it just the right "oomph."
Legend has it that a fisherman, tired of his wife's cooking, devised this recipe. As
he sat down to eat he mumbled "Anna, damn her" and from then on this was
"Anadama" bread.

	Small	Medium	Large
water	5⁄8 cup	1 cup-1½ tbs.	1¼ cups
molasses	2 tbs.	2½ tbs.	¼ cup
margarine/butter	½ tbs.	⅔ tbs.	1 tbs.
salt	⅓ tsp.	½ tsp.	¾ tsp.
cornmeal (yellow)	2 tbs.	2½ tbs.	¼ cup
bread flour	1½ cups	2 cups	3 cups
yeast	1 tsp.	1½ tsp.	2½ tsp.

CHRISTMAS ANISE BREAD

The flavor of anise adds a lot to this bread but is not overwhelming. If you want a stronger tasting bread, you may safely double the amount of anise and other spices.

	Small	Medium	Large
milk	½ cup	⅔ cup	1 cup
margarine/butter	2 tbs.	2½ tbs.	¼ cup
sugar	¾ tbs.	1 tbs.	1½ tbs.
salt	⅓ tsp.	½ tsp.	¾ tsp.
anise	¾ tsp.	1 tsp.	1½ tsp.
mace	dash	dash	⅛ tsp.
nutmeg	dash	dash	⅛ tsp.
grated lemon peel	⅓ tsp.	½ tsp.	¾ tsp.
grated orange peel	⅓ tsp.	½ tsp.	¾ tsp.
bread flour	1½ cups	2 cups	3 cups
nonfat dry milk	1½ tbs.	2 tbs.	3 tbs.
yeast	1 tsp.	1½ tsp.	2½ tsp.

CHRISTMAS BREAD

A strong, hearty bread for Christmas or any morning. Also wonderful with soup or stew.

	Small	Medium	Large
water	½ cup	¾ cup	1 cup
molasses	2 ½ tbs.	¼ cup	5 tbs.
honey	1⅓ tbs.	2 tbs.	2⅔ tbs.
margarine/butter	⅔ tbs.	1 tbs.	1⅓ tbs.
salt	⅔ tsp.	1 tsp.	1⅓ tsp.
oats	3 tbs.	⅓ cup	6 tbs.
bread flour	1⅔ cups	2½ cups	3⅓ cups
yeast	1 tsp.	1½ tsp.	2½ tsp.

COFFEE SPICE BREAD

Similar in taste to a brown bread and a great way to use up that leftover coffee — regular or decaf!

	Small	Medium	Large
leftover coffee	½ cup	⅔ cup	1 cup
vegetable oil	2 tbs.	2½ tbs.	¼ cup
egg	½	¾	1
sugar	1½ tbs.	2 tbs.	3 tbs.
salt	½ tsp.	⅔ tsp.	1 tsp.
cinnamon	½ tsp.	⅔ tsp.	1 tsp.
ground cloves	dash	⅛ tsp.	¼ tsp.
allspice	dash	⅛ tsp.	¼ tsp.
bread flour	1½ cups	2 cups	3 cups
yeast	1 tsp.	1½ tsp.	2½ tsp.

DOUGH CYCLE

BRIOCHE

These make marvelous coffee rolls — very rich texture. Worth using butter instead of margarine. Be sure to make plenty, as people will go back for seconds and even thirds!

	Small (8)	Medium (12)	Large (16)
milk	⅔ cup	1 cup	1⅓ cup
butter	2½ tbs.	4 tbs.	5 tbs.
eggs	1½	2	2½
sugar	2 tbs.	3 tbs.	¼ cup
salt	1 tsp.	1½ tsp.	2 tsp.
bread flour	2 cups	3 cups	4 cups
yeast	1 tsp.	1½ tsp.	2½ tsp.

Divide dough into 8, 12, or 16 large balls and an equal number of small balls. Place large balls of dough into muffin tins; press down in the center of each one to form an indentation into which you place a small ball of dough. Let rise for about 40 minutes. Brush tops with a mixture of 1 beaten egg and 1 tbs. sugar; bake in a preheated 375° oven for 15 to 20 minutes.

CROISSANTS

Making croissants was, pleasantly, not as difficult as one would think from the length of the directions. If you try this at least once, you will make them many times because you will see how easy it really is.The making of croissants is time-consuming; however, most of the time involved is actually in the dough rising or its being chilled. Should you decide to make them using the minimum amount of time allowed, you will need approximately 5½ hours. If you desire hot croissants in the morning, you'll need to start the process about 3 hours before refrigerating the dough overnight; and then approximately 1 hour in the morning.

	Small (12)	**Medium (16)**	**Large (24)**
milk	¾ cup	1⅛ cups	1½ cups
vegetable oil	2 tsp.	1 tbs.	1⅓ tbs.
sugar	1⅓ tsp.	2 tsp.	2⅔ tsp.
salt	1 tsp.	1½ tsp.	2 tsp.
all purpose flour	1⅔ cups	2½ cups	3⅓ cups
yeast	1 tsp.	1½ tsp.	2½ tsp.

Have ready but do not put in the machine:
cold butter   ⅔ cup   1 cup   1⅓ cups

Allow the dough to sit in the machine past the "stop time" with the lid down, so that the total first-rising time should be at least 2 to 2½ hours.

Cover the dough, right in the pan, and put it in the refrigerator for a minimum of 20 minutes.

Using a lightly floured plastic cutting board, a baking pan or any other rectangular item onto which you can roll the dough and pick the whole thing up for refrigeration; roll the dough out into a rectangular shape.

While the dough rests just a few seconds, knead the butter while holding it under cold running water. You should be able to make it into a ball easily. Spread the butter over the rectangle of dough, using a flat utensil such as a pastry knife or spatula. Leave about ¼ to ½ inch unbuttered around the edges.

Fold the dough into thirds, much as you would fold an 8½ x 11 piece of paper to fit into a business envelope.

Roll the dough into another rectangle, fold it into thirds and repeat again so that the dough has been rolled and folded a total of 3 times.

Cover the dough with plastic wrap loosely and refrigerate for a minimum of 1½ hours, or overnight if you want croissants in the morning.

Repeat the procedure for rolling dough into a rectangle and folding 3 more times. You may need to sprinkle flour on the dough and/or rolling pin for ease of rolling.

Roll the dough into another rectangle and cut into squares (about 4-5 inches, depending on the size of croissant you want). Then cut each square in half, forming a triangle. Roll each triangle into a crescent shape and place on a well greased baking sheet.

Chill for 20 to 30 minutes. Then bake in a preheated 400° oven for 10 minutes, drop the temperature to 350° and bake for another 10 to 15 minutes until done.

Variation: ALMOND CROISSANTS

Mix with the cold butter:
almond paste	2 tbs.	3 tbs.	¼ cup

Brush the top of the ready-to-be-baked croissants with an egg white and sprinkle with slivered almonds.

ALMOND BUTTER CRESCENTS

About half of my testers said these were just as good as the croissants. They are extremely simple to make, too.

	Small (6)	Medium (8)	Large (12)
milk	6 tbs.	2/3 cup	3/4 cup
butter	1/2 cup	3/4 cup	1 cup
almond extract	1 tsp.	1 1/2 tsp.	2 tsp.
almond paste	1 tbs.	1 1/2 tbs.	2 tbs.
eggs	2	2 1/2	3
sugar	1/4 cup	5 tbs.	1/2 cup
salt	1/4 tsp.	1/3 tsp.	1/2 tsp.
all purpose flour	2 cups	3 cups	4 cups
yeast	1 tsp.	1 1/2 tsp.	2 1/2 tsp.

Filling:

melted butter	¼ cup	5 tbs.	½ cup
almond extract	½ tsp.	¾ tsp.	1 tsp.

   The dough itself is extremely sticky and you will need to use a little flour for kneading when you take it out of the machine. Knead the dough very lightly and roll into 1 or 2 circles (depending on size of recipe you are making). Brush mixture of melted butter and almond extract on top of circle. Cut circle into 6 to 8 pieces, as you would a pie. Roll each piece from wide end to tip of triangle so that it forms a crescent. Place on a cornmeal-covered baking sheet, cover and let rise for approximately 1 hour. Bake at 400° for about 15 minutes, watching carefully to avoid burning.

CROISSANT LOAF

This loaf has flaky layers similar to croissants. Delicious.

	Small	Medium	Large
water	6 tbs.	2/3 cup	3/4 cup
margarine/butter	1¾ tbs.	2½ tbs.	3¼ tbs.
vanilla extract	2/3 tsp.	1 tsp.	1⅓ tsp.
eggs	1½	2	2½
sugar	2½ tbs.	¼ cup	5 tbs.
salt	½ tsp.	¾ tsp.	1 tsp.
all purpose flour	2 cups	3 cups	4 cups
yeast	1½ tsp.	2½ tsp.	3½ tsp.

For spreading over dough:

	Small	Medium	Large
butter/margarine	2 tbs.	3 tbs.	¼ cup

Roll dough into a ½" thick rectangle.

Cut half the butter or margarine into small pieces and place in the middle third of the dough. Fold one third over onto the top of the butter. Place the remaining butter, cut into small pieces, on top of the folded-over third and fold the remaining third over the butter. All butter is now encased in the dough.

Roll dough into another rectangle and fold into thirds, as you would a business letter. Wrap the whole thing loosely in waxed paper and refrigerate for approximately 20 minutes.

Roll the dough into a rectangle and fold into thirds, as above, 3 more times.

Now lightly knead dough, shaping into a ball which you then place in a greased loaf pan (or 2). Cover and let rise about 35 minutes until doubled in bulk.

Bake at 350° for 35 minutes or until golden brown.

CINNAMON ROLLS

These rolls are very good and are not overly sweet. About ⅔ of the testers liked them as is; the others wanted them sweeter. If you want a sweeter bun, make a glaze out of milk and powdered sugar to spread over the top while still warm.

	Small (9)	**Medium (14)**	**Large (18)**
milk	⅔ cup	1 cup	1⅓ cup
butter	1¼ tbs.	2 tbs.	2½ tbs.
eggs	1	1½	2
sugar	1⅓ tbs.	2 tbs.	2⅔ tbs.
salt	⅓ tsp.	½ tsp.	⅔ tsp.
all purpose flour	2 cups	3 cups	4 cups
yeast	1 tsp.	1½ tsp.	2½ tsp.

Filling

mix together:

sugar	2½ tbs.	¼ cup	5 tbs.
cinnamon	1 tbs.	1½ tbs.	2 tbs.
raisins, optional	⅓ cup	½ cup	⅔ cup

for brushing:

melted butter	1¼ tbs.	2 tbs.	2½ tbs.

Roll dough into a rectangle, brush with melted butter and spread the cinnamon mixture over that. Roll dough as a jellyroll and cut into slices of approximately 1½" in width. Place in a muffin tin, cover and let rise about 35 to 40 minutes. Brush top lightly with melted butter if desired. Bake at 400° for 20 to 25 minutes.

SWEET ROLLS

These are wonderful topped with jam. A special treat.

	Small (9)	Medium (12)	Large (15)
milk	½ cup	¾ cup	1 cup
margarine/butter	2½ tsp.	¼ cup	5 tbs.
eggs	½	1	1½
sugar	2½ tbs.	¼ cup	5 tbs.
salt	½ tsp.	¾ tsp.	1 tsp.
all purpose flour	2 cups	3 cups	4 cups
yeast	1 tsp.	1½ tsp.	2½ tsp.

After completion of dough cycle, shape into appropriate number of balls and place in muffin tins. Cover and let rise about 1 hour; bake at 350° for 20 minutes until done.

PARKER HOUSE DINNER ROLLS

Now synonymous with American dinner rolls, these were originated by The Parker House in Boston.

	Small (8)	Medium (12)	Large (16)
milk	2/3 cup	1 cup	1 1/3 cups
margarine/butter	1 1/4 tbs.	2 tbs.	2 1/2 tbs.
eggs	1/2	1	1 1/2
sugar	2 tsp.	1 tbs.	1 1/3 tbs.
salt	1/3 tsp.	1/2 tsp.	2/3 tsp.
all purpose flour	1 2/3 cups	2 1/2 cups	3 1/3 cups
yeast	2 1/2 tsp.	2 1/2 tsp.	2 1/2 tsp.

After completion of dough cycle, knead dough by hand for approximately 5 minutes. Roll out and cut with a biscuit cutter (or cup). Brush with melted butter (1/4 cup +/- depending on dough amount). Fold circles in half and place in buttered muffin tins. Cover and let rise 35 to 45 minutes. Brush tops with a beaten egg and bake at 400° for 25 to 30 minutes.

HAMBURGER/HOT DOG ROLLS

These are the best. Make plenty and freeze the extras for the next time, if you have any left, that is!

	Small (8)	Medium (12)	Large (16)
water	⅔ cup	1 cup	1⅓ cups
margarine/butter	1¼ tbs.	2 tbs.	2½ tbs.
sugar	1⅓ tbs.	2 tbs.	2⅔ tbs.
salt	1¼ tsp.	2 tsp.	2½ tsp.
bread flour	2 cups	3 cups	4 cups
nonfat dry milk	2 tbs.	3 tbs.	¼ cup
yeast	1 tsp.	1½ tsp.	2½ tsp.

Punch dough down and let rest for 20 minutes. Divide into appropriate number of balls, make bun shapes and flatten. Let rise for 1 hour; bake at 375° for 20 minutes or until done.

Wonderful as is, but if you like extras, try adding 1, 1½ or 2 tbs. of one of the following to the dough: sesame seeds, poppy seeds, chives, minced onion. You may also brush the tops of the buns with a beaten egg and sprinkle on sesame seeds immediately prior to baking.

SANDWICH ROLLS

These are wonderful hot out of the oven whether you make sandwiches with them or not.

	Small (8)	Medium (12)	Large (16)
water	1 cup-1½ tbs.	1¼ cups	1⅔ cups
vegetable oil	1⅓ tbs.	2 tbs.	2⅔ tbs.
sugar	1⅓ tsp.	2 tsp.	2⅔ tsp.
salt	1 tsp.	1½ tsp.	2 tsp.
bread flour	2 cups	3 cups	4 cups
nonfat dry milk or			
buttermilk powder	3 tbs.	⅓ cup	6 tbs.
yeast	1 tsp.	1½ tsp.	2½ tsp.

Divide into balls, shape into rolls and let rise for 40 to 50 minutes. Bake at 375° for 20 minutes or until done.

WHOLE WHEAT SANDWICH ROLLS

Wonderfully tasty as well as nutritious.

	Small (8)	Medium (12)	Large (16)
water	1 cup-1½ tbs.	1¼ cups	1⅔ cups
vegetable oil	1⅓ tbs.	2 tbs.	2⅔ tbs.
honey	2 tsp.	1 tbs.	1⅓ tbs.
salt	1 tsp.	1½ tsp.	2 tsp.
whole wheat flour	⅔ cup	1 cup	1⅓ cups
wheat/oat bran	1¼ tbs.	2 tbs.	2½ tbs.
wheat germ	2½ tbs.	¼ cup	5 tbs.
bread flour	1 cup+1½ tbs.	1¾ cups	2⅓ cups
nonfat dry milk	2½ tbs.	¼ cup	5 tbs.
yeast	1 tsp.	1½ tsp.	2½ tsp.

Divide into balls, make desired shape of rolls and let rise for 50 to 60 minutes. Bake at 375° for 20 minutes or until done.

CHALLAH

The traditional Challah is braided, but this recipe may also be baked using the regular setting. Challah is a very light and wonderful tasting bread.

	Small	Medium	Large
water	⅔ cup	1 cup	1⅓ cup
eggs	1½	2	2½
vegetable oil	1⅓ tbs.	2 tbs.	2⅔ tbs.
sugar	1⅓ tbs.	2 tbs.	2⅔ tbs.
salt	1 tsp.	1½ tsp.	2 tsp.
bread flour	2 cups	3 cups	4 cups
yeast	1 tsp.	1½ tsp.	2½ tsp.

Divide dough into 3 pieces; roll them into strands and braid them. Cover and let rise for approximately 45 minutes. Brush top with a beaten egg and sprinkle with poppy seeds, if you wish. Bake at 375° for 45 minutes.

LITHUANIAN COFFEE BREAD

Tom and Rasa, friends of Lithuanian descent, said this tasted just like the coffee breads their mothers used to make.

	Small	Medium	Large
bread dough:			
milk	⅓ cup	½ cup	⅔ cup
margarine/butter	2½ tbs.	4 tbs.	5 tbs.
eggs	1½	2	2½
egg yolk	1	1	1
vanilla	⅔ tsp.	1 tsp.	1⅓ tsp.
salt	⅓ tsp.	½ tsp.	⅔ tsp.
sugar	⅓ cup	½ cup	⅔ cup
grated lemon peel	⅔ tsp.	1 tsp.	1⅓ tsp.
bread flour	2 cups	3 cups	4 cups
yeast	1 tsp.	1½ tsp.	2½ tsp.

filling:

sugar	2½ tbs.	¼ cup	5 tbs.
chopped walnuts	2½ tbs.	¼ cup	5 tbs.
raisins	⅓ cup	½ cup	⅔ cup

After completion of dough cycle, divide and roll dough out into three rectangles. Spread ⅓ of mixed filling ingredients onto middle of each rectangle and fold dough over it to encase it. Braid rectangles together and place in a bread loaf pan. Let rise about 30 minutes. Brush with beaten egg. Bake in a preheated 400° oven for 40 to 45 minutes until brown.

HOT CROSS BUNS

You needn't wait for Easter to come around to enjoy these — with or without the frosting cross. Absolutely delicious.

	Small (8)	**Medium (12)**	**Large (16)**
milk	½ cup	¾ cup	1 cup
eggs	1¼	2	2½
margarine/butter	2 tbs.	3 tbs.	¼ cup
sugar	2½ tbs.	¼ cup	5 tbs.
salt	⅓ tsp.	½ tsp.	⅔ tsp.
cinnamon	⅔ tsp.	1 tsp.	1⅓ tsp.
all purpose flour	2 cups	3 cups	4 cups
yeast	1 tsp.	1½ tsp.	2½ tsp.
raisins	½ cup	¾ cup	1 cup

About 5 minutes prior to the end of the dough kneading cycle, add raisins or knead them in by hand at the completion of the cycle. After a short kneading, let the dough rest for about 10 minutes. Cut dough into desired amount of pieces, shape each one into a ball and place in a greased baking dish. Cover and let rise about 35 minutes or until doubled in bulk. Brush with a mixture of egg yolk and 2 tsp. water. Bake at 375° for 20 to 25 minutes.

If desired, after buns are completely cool, drizzle in the shape of a cross, a mixture of: 1 cup confectioners' sugar, 1/2 tsp. vanilla and 1 tbs. milk.

PITA BREAD

This is a definite "must try." Well worth the few minutes involved to make. Easy to have done in time for lunch sandwiches.

	Small (6)	Medium (8)	Large (10)
water	⅔ cup	1 cup	1⅓ cups
olive oil	1⅓ tbs.	2 tbs.	2⅔ tbs.
sugar	2 tsp.	1 tbs.	1⅓ tbs.
salt	⅔ tsp.	1 tsp.	1⅓ tsp.
bread flour	1 cup	1½ cups	2 cups
whole wheat flour	⅔ cup	1 cup	1⅓ cups
yeast	1 tsp.	1½ tsp.	2½ tsp.

Upon completion of dough cycle, divide dough into the appropriate number of pieces and roll into balls. Let rise about 20 minutes. Flatten each ball into a disk, rolling each one into a circle of approximately 6". Place on a baking sheet and bake in a preheated 500° oven for 8 to 10 minutes.

BREAD STICKS

Far better than the ones you buy in the store. Bake enough to keep on hand. Each of the different toppings changes the flavor of the sticks — try them all.

	Small	Medium	Large
water	⅔ cup	1 cup	1⅓ cups
margarine/butter	¾ tbs.	1 tbs.	1¼ tbs.
sugar	2 tsp.	1 tbs.	1⅓ tbs.
salt	⅔ tsp.	1 tsp.	1⅓ tsp.
bread flour	2 cups	3 cups	4 cups
nonfat dry milk	2 tbs.	3 tbs.	¼ cup
yeast	1 tsp.	1½ tsp.	2½ tsp.

Cut dough into small pieces and roll them into ropes. Cover and let rise 20 minutes. Brush each one with a mixture of 1 egg white and 1 tablespoon of water. Sprinkle on coarse salt, sesame seeds, poppy seeds, anise or other desired topping. Bake at 400° for 15 minutes or until golden brown. The shorter the baking time, the softer they are; the longer the baking time, the crunchier.

CRUSTY PIZZA DOUGH

My family was devastated when the local pizza parlor closed, forcing us to start making our own pizzas. Pizza making has now become a family adventure. One of our favorites includes leftover turkey and frozen mixed vegetables as toppings. Truly a great way to use leftovers! Small will make one 14" pizza medium will make one 14"-16" pizza depending on thickness of crust large will make two 14" pizzas.

	Small	Medium	Large
water	⅔ cup	1 cup	1⅓ cups
olive oil	1¼ tsp.	2 tsp.	2½ tsp.
salt	⅓ tsp.	½ tsp.	⅔ tsp.
all purpose flour	1 cup	1½ cups	2 cups
whole wheat flour	1 cup	1½ cups	2 cups
yeast	1 tsp.	1½ tsp.	2½ tsp.

Roll dough into rectangle or circle, depending on pan to be used. Place on pan and turn excess under, forming a crust on the side. Brush very lightly with olive oil. Cover and let rise about 30 minutes. Top with pizza sauce and desired toppings. Place in a cold oven, turn temperature up to 450° and bake until crust is brown and cheese is melted, 30 to 45 minutes.

CHEESE PIZZA DOUGH

The cheese gives it an interesting taste and texture.

	Small	Medium	Large
water	2/3 cup	1 cup	1 1/3 cups
olive oil	2 tsp.	1 tbs.	1 1/3 tbs.
shredded mozzarella	1/3 cup	1/2 cup	2/3 cup
salt	1/3 tsp.	1/2 tsp.	2/3 tsp.
all purpose flour	1 cup	1 1/2 cups	2 cups
whole wheat flour	1 cup	1 1/2 cups	2 cups
yeast	1 tsp.	1 1/2 tsp.	2 1/2 tsp.

Roll dough into rectangle or circle, depending on pan to be used. Place on pan and turn excess under, forming a crust on the side. Brush very lightly with olive oil. Cover and let rise about 30 minutes. Top with pizza sauce and desired toppings. Place in a cold oven, turn temperature up to 450° and bake until crust is brown and cheese is melted, 30 to 45 minutes.

BAGELS

I was ready to give up on a bagel recipe until my frustration finally led me to a local bagel bakery where they shared some hints with me.

	Small (8)	Medium (12)	Large (16)
water	2/3 cup	1 cup	1 1/3 cups
honey	1 tbs.	1 1/2 tbs.	2 tbs.
salt	1 tsp.	1 1/2 tsp.	2 tsp.
whole wheat flour	2/3 cup	1 cup	1 1/3 cups
bread flour	1 1/3 cups	2 cups	2 2/3 cups
yeast	1 tsp.	1 1/2 tsp.	2 1/2 tsp.

Let the machine knead the dough once, and then let the dough rise 20 minutes only in the machine. Even if your cycle runs longer, simply remove dough after 20 minutes and turn off the machine. Divide the dough into the appropriate number of pieces. Each piece should be rolled into a rope and made into a circle, pressing the ends together. You may find it necessary to wet one end slightly to help seal the ends together.

Place these on a well greased baking sheet, cover and let rise only 15 to 20 minutes. Meanwhile, bring to a slight boil in a *nonaluminum pan*, (I use a cast iron frying pan), about 2 inches of water. Carefully lower about 3 or 4 bagels at a time into the water, cooking for about 30 seconds on each side. Remove bagels, drain on a towel, sprinkle with poppy seeds, sesame seeds or dried onion bits if desired and place on the greased baking sheet. Bake in a preheated 550° oven for 8 minutes.

PRETZELS

I bet you can't eat just one!

	Small (12)	Medium (18)	Large (24)
water	⅔ cup	1 cup	1⅓ cups
margarine/butter	1¼ tbs.	2 tbs.	2½ tbs.
sugar	2 tsp.	1 tbs.	1⅓ tbs.
salt	⅓ tsp.	½ tsp.	⅔ tsp.
all purpose flour	2 cups	3 cups	4 cups
yeast	1 tsp.	1½ tsp.	2½ tsp.

Cut dough into short strips, roll into ropes and shape into pretzels. Cover and let rise about 45 minutes.

In a cast iron or other *nonaluminum* pan, bring almost to a boil 4 cups of water and 5 teaspoons of baking soda. Gently place (by hand or slotted spoon) the pretzels into the water for approximately 1 minute, turning once. Do not let water come to a full boil. Remove pretzels and place on a greased baking sheet. Sprinkle with coarse salt (also called sea salt or Kosher salt). Bake at 475° for about 12 minutes.

MAIL ORDER & SOURCES OF INGREDIENTS GUIDE

Ancient Harvest
Quinoa Corporation
24248 Crenshaw Blvd., Suite 220
Torrance, CA 90505
(213) 530-8666

Quinoa grains, flour and products. If you cannot locate quinoa, ask your health food store to contact company to order.

Arrowhead Mills, Inc.
Box 866
Hereford, TX 79045
(806) 364-0730

A wide variety of grains and flours. Mail order catalog available. Supplier to health food stores.

Ener-G Foods
P. O. Box 84487
Seattle, WA 98124-5787
(800) 331-5222

Mail order catalog and wholesale supplier of items such as egg powder.

Garden Spot Distributors
438 White Oak Road
New Holland, PA 17557
(800) 829-5100

Mail order of a wide variety of organic and chemical-free whole grains, flours, cereals, dried fruit, nuts and wheat-free and gluten-free ingredients.

Great Valley Mills
RD 3 Box 1111
Barto , PA 19504
(800) 688-6455

Mail order of stone ground flours and other items from Pennsylvania Dutch farms.

Morgan's Mills
RD2 Box 4602
Union, ME 04862
(207) 785-4900

Mail order catalog of stone ground flour, natural and gourmet foods.

Walnut Acres
Penns Creek, PA 17862
(800) 433-3998

Mail order catalog from this organic farm; flours, grains and many other items.

The Vermont Country Store
P. O. Box 3000
Manchester Center, VT 05255-3000
(802) 362-4647

Mail order catalog of stone ground flours and cereals as well as other items.

King Arthur Flour
Rrt. #2 Box 56
Norwich, VT 05055
(802) 649-3881

Mail order catalog of flours, grains and other items.

NUTRITIONAL COMPARISONS

	Calories	Protein (grams)	Carbo-hydrates
Flours and Meals (½ cup)			
All purpose	200	5.5	43.0
Amaranth	200	8.0	35.0
Barley	200	7.0	43.0
Bread	200	7.0	41.5
Buckwheat	190	7.0	41.0
Cornmeal-Blue	210	6.0	41.0
Cornmeal-Yellow	200	4.0	44.0
Gluten-Vital	200	30.0	18.0
Millet	185	6.0	41.0
Oat	200	7.0	43.0
Quinoa	200	9.0	35.0
Rice	200	4.0	44.0
Rye	190	9.0	39.0
Soy	250	20.0	18.0
Teff	200	7.0	41.0

	Calories	Protein (grams)	Carbo-hydrates
Triticale	190	7.0	41.0
Whole Wheat	200	8.0	40.0

Milk Products (one cup fresh or powder mixed with water equal to)

	Calories	Protein (grams)	Carbo-hydrates
Buttermilk	100	8.0	12.0
Buttermilk powder	79	7.5	10.7
Nonfat dry milk	80	8.0	12.0
Skim milk	85	8.0	12.0
Whole milk	150	8.0	11.0

Egg (one egg or equivalent)

	Calories	Protein (grams)	Carbo-hydrates
Whole	80	6.0	1.0
White	15	3.0	Tr
Yolk	65	3.0	Tr
Substitute	60	6.0	3.0
Egg Powder	15	0.0	3.0

PERCENTAGE OF U.S. RECOMMENDED DAILY ALLOWANCES
Flours (½ cup serving)

	Calcium	Iron	Thia-mine	Ribo-flavin	Niacin
All purpose	2	25	45	25	30
Amaranth	10	80	*	8	4
Barley	2	10	15	2	15
Bread	2	25	45	25	30
Buckwheat	2	8	20	6	8
Gluten-Vital	*	12	4	*	8
Millet	2	20	30	15	6
Oat	2	15	30	2	2
Quinoa	6	26	10	10	4
Rice	2	6	10	2	15
Rye	4	15	25	8	8
Soy	10	30	25	10	6
Teff	10	25	15	4	4
Triticale	2	8	15	4	8
Whole Wheat	2	10	2	6	15

BIBLIOGRAPHY

Gelles, Carol. *The Complete Whole Grain Cookbook*. New York: Donald I. Fine, 1989

Goldbeck, Nikki and David. *Goldbecks' Guide to Good Food*. New York: New American Library (NAL), 1987

Greene, Bert. *The Grains Cookbook*. New York: Workman Publishing, 1988

Wood, Rebecca. *The Whole Foods Encyclopedia*. New York: Prentice Hall, 1988

U. S. Department of Agriculture. *Nutritive Value of Foods*. Home and Garden Bulletin Number 72. Revised 1981.

Von Welanetz, Diana & Paul. *The Von Welanetz Guide to Ethnic Ingredients*. Los Angeles: J.P. Tarcher, Inc., 1982

RESOURCES

Arrowhead Mills, Inc., Hereford, TX

Fleischmann's Yeast, Parsippany, NJ

The Pillsbury Company, Minneapolis, MN

INDEX

SERVE CREATIVE, EASY, NUTRITIOUS MEALS WITH NITTY GRITTY® COOKBOOKS

The Bread Machine Cookbook
The Bread Machine Cookbook II
The Sandwich Maker Cookbook
The Juicer Book
Bread Baking (traditional), revised
The Kid's Cookbook, revised
The Kid's Microwave Cookbook
15-Minute Meals for 1 or 2
Recipes for the 9x13 Pan
Turkey, the Magic Ingredient
Chocolate Cherry Tortes and Other Lowfat Delights
Lowfat American Favorites
Lowfat International Cuisine

The Hunk Cookbook
Now That's Italian!
Fabulous Fiber Cookery
Low Salt, Low Sugar, Low Fat Desserts
What's for Breakfast?
Healthy Cooking on the Run
Healthy Snacks for Kids
Creative Soups & Salads
Quick & Easy Pasta Recipes
Muffins, Nut Breads and More
The Barbecue Book
The Wok
New Ways with Your Wok
Quiche & Soufflé Cookbook

Easy Microwave Cooking
Cooking for 1 or 2
Meals in Minutes
New Ways to Enjoy Chicken
Favorite Seafood Recipes
No Salt, No Sugar, No Fat Cookbook
New International Fondue Cookbook
Extra-Special Crockery Pot Recipes
Favorite Cookie Recipes
Authentic Mexican Cooking
Fisherman's Wharf Cookbook
The Creative Lunch Box

Write or call for our free catalog.
Bristol Publishing Enterprises, Inc.
P.O. Box 1737, San Leandro, CA 94577
(800)346-4889; in California (510)895-4461

For information about Donna German's *Bread Machine Newsletter*, write to:
976 Houston Northcutt Blvd, Suite 3, Mount Pleasant, SC 29464